THE

Dust of Life

America's Children
Abandoned in Vietnam

THE
Dust of Life

America's Children
Abandoned in Vietnam

ROBERT S. MCKELVEY

UNIVERSITY OF WASHINGTON PRESS

Seattle and London

*This publication was supported in part by the
Donald R. Ellegood International Publications Endowment.*

Copyright © 1999 by the University of Washington Press
Printed in the United States of America

All rights reserved. No part of this publication may be reproduced or
transmitted in any form or by any means, electronic or mechanical,
including photocopy, recording, or any information storage or retrieval
system, without permission in writing from the publisher.

Library of Congress Cataloging-in-Publication Data
McKelvey, Robert S.
The dust of life : America's children abandoned in Vietnam /
Robert S. McKelvey.
p.   cm.
Includes bibliographical references and index.
ISBN 0-295-97825-2 (alk. paper) (cloth)
ISBN 0-295-97836-8 pbk.
1. Amerasians—Vietnam.
2. Children of military personnel—Vietnam.
3. Abandoned children—Vietnam.
4. Amerasians—United States.
5. Vietnamese Americans.
I. Title.
DS556.45.A43M35   1999   99-22670
305.8'0420597—DC21   CIP

The paper used in this publication is acid-free and recycled from 10 percent
post-consumer and at least 50 percent pre-consumer waste. It meets the
minimum requirments of American National Standard for Information
Sciences—Permanence of Paper for Printed Library Materials,
ANSI Z39.48–1984. ♾ ♻

This book is dedicated to my family.
To my mother, Margaret McKelvey Snider;
my father, Robert S. McKelvey, Jr.;
my wife, Jill Roman;
my daughter, Cara McKelvey;
and my son, Lowell McKelvey.
Their love and support over the years
have made all the difference.

Contents

Preface

I HAVE BEEN LEARNING ABOUT VIETNAMESE AMERASIANS FOR the past nine years, and have often been asked how I became interested in them. Had I myself, perhaps, fathered an Amerasian child during my military service in Vietnam? While my interest in Amerasians did develop from a love affair, it was one of a different kind; a love affair with Vietnam, its culture, and its people.

In 1964 I was studying German at the Goethe Institut in Lüneburg, Germany. One warm summer day, as I sat in a city park reading the *Frankfurter Allgemeine,* I came across an account of an attack by North Vietnamese torpedo boats on a U.S. Navy destroyer in the Gulf of Tonkin. Where, I wondered, was the Gulf of Tonkin? Where was Vietnam? Like many other Americans, I was soon to learn much more about these and many other locations in Southeast Asia.

In 1965, during my senior year at Harvard, I read of Marine landings across Red Beach in Da Nang, South Vietnam. Driven by a desire to escape temporarily from the confines of academic life, I applied for a commission in the U.S. Marine Corps. In a piece of youthful illogic, I did not see a connection between this decision and the possibility that I might have to participate in the distant, rapidly expanding war. During boot camp that summer I began to meet veterans of the Vietnam conflict and gleaned a confusing picture of U.S. efforts to support a democratic country fighting communism. I was still not particularly concerned that the war might touch my life. Along with many other Americans, I assumed it would soon be over, that the United States would win, and that I would not have to go. This belief was reinforced by the fact that I had a year's study leave from the Marine Corps to pursue a fellowship at a German university and would be on inactive duty status until late 1967. Surely the war would be over by then.

However, when in September of 1967 I returned to the Marine Corps's Basic School in Quantico, Virginia, the war was in full bloom and the Marine Corps was playing a major role in it. All of our training during that fall and winter was skewed toward participation in the conflict, including mock assaults across frozen paddy fields in northern Virginia, and each one of us assumed he would soon be there. I received a couple of reprieves along the way: first a three-month tour at Fort Sill, the Army's artillery school in Lawton, Oklahoma; then an eight-month hiatus at the Defense Language Institute in Monterey, California. Even though I was learning Vietnamese, the length of the course again gave me hope that the war would end before I got there. Meanwhile, I enjoyed my studies of the Vietnamese language and culture immensely. The only cultures I knew well were those of the United States and Germany, where I had spent considerable time studying German language and literature. The language and culture of Vietnam were a world apart. Aside from some French words adopted over a century of colonial rule and a few recent additions from the American military vocabulary, there was nothing even remotely familiar about Vietnamese, a tonal language rendered into Roman script by Jesuit missionaries in the seventeenth century. Vietnamese culture was equally unfamiliar. I learned of ancestor veneration, ghosts and spirits, gods of villages and temples, and the predominant religion of Vietnam, Buddhism. Despite my fear of the war, I was fascinated by Vietnam and its ancient culture.

In August 1969 I was ordered to Vietnam to begin my thirteen-month tour of duty. I spent the first few months working as a fire direction officer in an artillery battalion providing support to the infantry regiments guarding Da Nang and its enormous air base. I had little opportunity to use my newly acquired language skills or to learn more about Vietnamese culture. Instead I spent my days and nights plotting artillery fires into the rice paddies and mountains west of Da Nang. Then an opportunity arose to become the battalion's, and later the regiment's, S-5 or Civil Affairs Officer. This was a job much more to my liking, charged with "winning the hearts and minds" of the Vietnamese population in our area. I am not sure how many Vietnamese hearts and minds I won during the next seven or eight months, but Vietnam certainly won mine.

It is difficult to explain why I came to love Vietnam so much. Perhaps, as some Vietnamese friends have suggested, I was Vietnamese in a past life. However, I think it had something to do with my perception of the all-embracing character of Vietnamese culture; the sense that life exists before and after death, that both animate and inanimate objects are imbued with life, and that each of us, in his, her, or its own way, belongs to, and is a part of, God's creation. I was also enthralled by the beauty of the countryside and the quiet rhythms of Vietnamese life, dominated by the planting and cultivation of rice according to a pattern established thousands of years before. Whatever the reason, I fell in love with the place, and that love has never left me.

After my tour of duty was over, I returned home and decided to study medicine. My intention was to become a general practitioner and return to live and work in Vietnam. However, the United States' abandonment of the Republic of South Vietnam in 1973 and the Communist victory on April 30, 1975, seemed to banish Vietnam from the thoughts of Americans. In the late 1970s we read of boat people and of Vietnam's border wars with Cambodia and China, but other concerns soon occupied our minds. Those of us who had fought there seldom spoke of it—it was not a popular topic at social gatherings—and most chose simply to get on with their lives. I was drawn to psychiatry, and eventually child psychiatry, and put aside my earlier plans to return to Vietnam.

Then, in the mid- and late 1980s, Vietnam again began to intrude into our consciousness. Movies like *Platoon, Full Metal Jacket,* and *Gardens of Stone* caused us to revisit our participation there, portraying those of us who had fought in the war less as evildoers than as victims of a confusing and misguided catastrophe. I began to reflect on my own involvement and wrote a piece, later published in the *Journal of the American Medical Association,* about a heartbreaking experience during which I witnessed the war's fatal collision with a Vietnamese family's life.[1] In 1988 a journalist, Laura Palmer, read the article and phoned to interview me for a column on Vietnam veterans she wrote for the *New York Daily News.* In the course of our conversation she mentioned that she was about to go back to Vietnam, where she had been a correspondent for several years during the war, to write a series of articles about Amerasians, the children born of unions between Americans and Vietnamese women.

I had not heard of Amerasians before, although stories about them were gradually beginning to appear in newspapers and periodicals. The picture that emerged was of wretched street children swarming around photographers in a park in the former Saigon. I did not know of the Amerasian Homecoming Act, a bill passed by Congress in December 1987 in a much-belated attempt to bring home America's children in Vietnam. As I read Laura Palmer's pieces about the Amerasians, and learned of their journey from the Amerasian Transit Center in Ho Chi Minh City to the Philippine Refugee Processing Center and finally to various cluster sites around the United States, an idea began to form in my mind. As an academic child psychiatrist, I was looking for a research project. What about a study of the mental health adjustment of Amerasians? The groundwork for such a study had already been laid by

---

1. Robert S. McKelvey, "Remembered Pain," *Journal of the American Medical Association* 260 (1988): 693.

Kirk Felsman and his colleagues at Dartmouth, who had studied Vietnamese Amerasians at the Philippine Refugee Processing Center.[2] In their report they suggested an extension of their study, evaluating Amerasians in Vietnam and then following them through the Philippines to the United States.

I must admit that my principal reason for wanting to conduct such a study was that it offered an opportunity to return to Vietnam. I had briefly considered traveling to Da Nang, and the nearby villages where I had worked during the war, to interview people I had known there about their lives since the war's end. However, I was told by medical school colleagues that such a project was too qualitative and not "scientific" enough. So a quantitative study of Amerasians, potentially publishable in a medical journal, seemed the next best thing. I found financial support for the project from the Vietnam Veterans of America and Baylor College of Medicine, and began the lengthy process of applying for a visa.

In 1989 the United States still did not have diplomatic relations with Vietnam, so U.S. citizens wishing to travel there had to secure a visa through the Vietnamese Mission to the United Nations in New York. This was a time-consuming process, involving several trips to the Mission to explain the purpose of my journey and be vetted by them. Not surprisingly, perhaps, for a people who had been at war for several decades, and who had not had the best of experiences with the United States, the Vietnamese seemed very suspicious of Americans wishing to travel to Vietnam. I wondered how they would receive a former Marine who had fought against them there, knew some Vietnamese, and wanted to return to conduct a "study." However, the process was a fascinating one, a real adventure, and brought back memories of the sadness and futility of the war. I remember particularly a party I at-

2. J. Kirk Felsman et al., *Vietnamese Amerasians: Practical Implications of Current Research* (Washington, D.C.: Office of Refugee Resettlement, Department of Health and Human Services, 1989).

tended for the Vietnamese ambassador to the United Nations. It struck me as enormously incongruous that we, who had been enemies, should now be attending a social gathering together. A poem I wrote at the time captures my sense of the sad irony of the event.

> Twenty years ago
> I saw your brothers,
> blood-smeared bodies,
> gray-green in death,
> naked and alone
> beneath a winter sky.
>
> Now we meet,
> you and I,
> smiling in our business suits,
> wishing one another well,
> champagne glasses in our hands
> instead of guns.
>
> What do we share?
> What is the fate
> of hate transformed by years?
> There are no tears
> in dry, blank eyes,
> only muted pain
> —so much lost,
> so little gained.[3]

Eventually I received confirmation that my visa had been approved and in June 1990 was off for a month's visit to Ho Chi Minh City and the Amerasian Transit Center.

3. Robert S. McKelvey, "At a Cocktail Party with the Vietnamese Ambassador to the United Nations," *Journal of the American Medical Association* 266 (1991):1896.

It is difficult to convey the complex mixture of anxiety, nostalgia, and excitement I felt as the Air France jumbo jet touched down at Tan Son Nhut Airport. I had last been there in February 1970, catching an "Air America" flight back to Da Nang after a brief visit to Saigon to purchase a rice mill for farmers in one of the villages where I worked. Then, the airport had been the busiest in the world, bustling with military jets taking off to bomb the surrounding countryside and provide American troops with close fire support, and commercial passenger jets ferrying GIs "in country," on R and R, or back to "the World" after a year in "the Nam." In 1990 it was a quiet place, the concrete revetments where Air Force "Phantom" jets once sheltered from Viet Cong mortars now overgrown with grass and empty except for an occasional rusting helicopter. What appeared to be an old U.S. military bus ferried us from the plane to the once-sparkling terminal, now dirty and worn, where tense, unfriendly Vietnamese customs officials searched every piece of luggage before releasing me into the hot and steamy June afternoon. Outside I was confronted by a throng of people, some waiting to meet passengers, others selling drinks and cigarettes, still others offering, in accents I had not heard for twenty years, to transport me into town in a "Numba One" cyclo, the traditional Vietnamese pedicab.

I finally selected a driver from the multitude assailing me and stepped into an old French taxi, remnant of an earlier war, for the ride into the city. The ancient car broke down half a mile from the airport in the midst of a tropical downpour, and my driver had to run back through the rain to find an operational vehicle. Waiting there in the stifling heat with doors locked and windows rolled up against some imagined danger, I was startled by a sharp rapping on the glass. Turning to confront the sound, I was greeted by the smiling face of a Vietnamese boy offering to sell me a pack of pornographic playing cards. Some things had changed little in the past twenty years.

The driver of the new taxi, taking advantage of what must have seemed the opportunity of a lifetime, charged me forty American dol-

lars for the journey downtown (the average yearly income in Vietnam
at that time was about $150). Arriving at the Foreign Affairs Bureau,
my host and sponsor for the next four weeks, I learned that the guest
house was closed and my room would not be available until Monday. I
would have to find another place to stay. Because I had recently re-
read Graham Greene's novel *The Quiet American,* the first hotel that
came to mind was the Majestic, where generations of war correspon-
dents once sipped drinks and discussed the latest battles. Like many
other buildings and streets in Ho Chi Minh City, the hotel's name had
been changed to reflect the nationalistic spirit of the new government.
It was now Cuu Long (Nine Dragons, the Vietnamese name for the
Mekong River). My driver, however, was old enough to remember its
former name, and so I spent my first night in Vietnam in this famous, if
dilapidated, French colonial hotel along the Saigon River at the end of
the former Freedom Street (now renamed Uprising). Here GIs once
walked arm in arm with their Vietnamese girl friends, dancing and
drinking the night away at "Maxim's" nightclub, before retiring to
nearby hotels for liaisons that may have produced some of the
Amerasians I had come to interview.

The next morning, after a breakfast of espresso and French baguettes, I walked along Uprising Street to the Foreign Affairs Bureau.
On the way I encountered many reminders of past wars and past re-
gimes. I passed the Caravelle Hotel, where I had stayed during my
1970 visit to Saigon, and came across the old French opera house, now
a movie theater. Across the street, where an immense statue of a charg-
ing South Vietnamese soldier had once stood, there was only a disused
fountain. Further on, past the Continental Hotel, traces of the French
colonial city's ambience appeared, with large trees, their trunks
painted a faded white, shading yellow government buildings, one of
which once housed the infamous Surete. Along the curb, etched in
tile, was the street's former French name, Rue Catinat. Catinat, then
Freedom, now Uprising Street begins at a graceful square framing Saigon's most famous landmark, the Cathedral of Our Lady. Inside this

lovely red brick structure, whose walls are lined with French and Vietnamese messages of thanks and supplication, is a stained glass window depicting Vietnamese peasants kneeling before a white European Virgin Mary. Behind the cathedral is April 30th Park, where Amerasians once thronged in front of the Foreign Affairs Bureau to present their petitions to anyone who would listen. Beyond the park is the former Presidential Palace (now Unification Hall), where Nguyen van Thieu and others presided over the erstwhile Republic of South Vietnam. And down the street in the opposite direction is the former American embassy, whose rooftop served as the precarious departure point for Americans leaving Saigon just ahead of North Vietnamese tanks and infantry on April 30, 1975.

At the Foreign Affairs Bureau I met the officials responsible for my stay and discussed plans to conduct research at the Amerasian Transit Center. I would live in the Bureau's Guest House and be driven out to the Transit Center each day in an air-conditioned government car. Translators would be supplied by the Bureau, and the staff of the Center would assist me in any way they could. The atmosphere of the meeting was polite, but tense, reflecting, it seemed to me, the continued hostility between the Vietnamese and U.S. governments and the deep mistrust each held for the other. Collecting my luggage from the Majestic Hotel, I moved into the Bureau's guest house and the next day began my first visit to the Transit Center.

The Center is located in District 11, not far from Tan Son Nhut Airport and directly across the street from the Dam Sen amusement park. It was "purpose-built" with U.S. funds in 1989 and early 1990 to house Amerasians and their families awaiting final approval of their applications and passage to the Philippines. Its buildings consist of several two-story, barrackslike structures, very comfortable by Vietnamese standards, set on a neatly maintained campus. The Center's director, Le van Thien, is a former Viet Cong guerrilla who fought for many years against both the French and the Americans in the famous tunnels of Cu Chi. He and his staff, and especially Mrs. Lien-Tam, the Center's associate director, were very hospitable and helpful to me on this and several subsequent visits to the Center. In the course of our work together they taught me a great deal about Amerasians and the life of Vietnam and its people, and I would like to think that we have become friends. I certainly owe them a tremendous debt of gratitude.

Acknowledgments

MANY PEOPLE IN VIETNAM AND THE UNITED STATES HAVE assisted and supported me in the preparation of this book. First and foremost, I would like to thank those Vietnamese Amerasians who shared their life stories with me and allowed me to share them with others. I am also deeply indebted to the staff of the Amerasian Transit Center in Ho Chi Minh City, and especially to its Director, Le van Thien, and its Associate Director, Nguyen Dieu Lien Tam, for their invaluable assistance during my visits there. Without their help, this book would not have been possible.

I owe a tremendous debt of gratitude to my research colleague and friend John Webb, with whom I have worked closely over the past eight years. He has played a major role in our past research about Vietnamese Amerasians, provided very useful suggestions for the structure of this book, and helped arrange my interviews with Amerasians in the United States.

I am also very grateful to Thien Kim Pham and Truong Van Nguyen for their invaluable contributions as interpreters and for the wisdom and guidance they provided in my attempts to understand Vietnamese culture and the challenges faced by Vietnamese adapting to life in the United States. I would like to acknowledge Ms. Pham's special contribution in interviewing "Minh," whose story appears in chapter 7, and who I was not able to interview personally.

My thanks to Miriam Landau in Perth, Western Australia, for reading and commenting on the original manuscript and for her continued interest in the book's progress. And a very special thank you to Associate Professor Victoria Burbank from the Anthropology Department at the University of Western Australia, who spent many hours reading the manuscript and advising me both on its content and on the complex ethical and moral challenges of faithfully representing the lives of other human beings.

Throughout this project my wife, Jill Roman, has provided enormous support and inspiration, traveling with me to Vietnam several times, discussing various aspects of the book, and maintaining a high level of confidence in my ability to get the job done. My son, Lowell, has also provided continuous and on-going support for the project, and helped me flesh out the original concept on a drive from Big Sky to Bozeman, Montana.

Finally, I am very grateful to the Hogg Foundation for Mental Health in Austin, Texas, for its support of this project and my previous work with Vietnamese Americans.

THE

Dust of Life

America's Children
Abandoned in Vietnam

1 / Who Are the
Vietnamese Amerasians?

VIETNAMESE AMERASIANS ARE A LIVING LEGACY OF AMERICA'S
longest and least popular war. The children of U.S. citizens and Vietnamese women, many Amerasians grew up in poverty as "half-breed"
(*con lai*) outcasts on the fringes of Vietnamese society. Discriminated
against for their mixed race and obvious connection to the American
enemy, Amerasians were often denied educational and employment
opportunities as children of "collaborators." Many were abandoned,
not only by their American fathers, but by their mothers and subsequent caretakers as well. Some survived as street children in Ho Chi
Minh City, others lived with their families in rural villages and provincial towns or became settlers in the harsh, isolated conditions of
Vietnam's "New Economic Zones." Although the Amerasians were
initially rejected as the responsibility of either the Vietnamese or the
U.S. government, American public interest in them was rekindled in
the 1980s by journalistic accounts of their fate, leading, in 1987,
to Congressional passage of what became known as the Amerasian
Homecoming Act. Under the conditions of the act, Amerasians and
their immediate family members are offered the opportunity to immigrate, at U.S. government expense, to the United States, where they
receive refugee entitlement benefits such as housing, health care, job
training, and English language instruction. Over 70,000 Amerasians
and their relatives have seized this opportunity to live in the United

3

States.[1] Others were either unwilling or unable to participate in the Amerasian Resettlement Program and continue to live in Vietnam. How many still remain is uncertain. I have heard estimates ranging from several hundred to several thousand. Their numbers are difficult to know, because many reportedly live in remote areas such as among the Montagnards or in the New Economic Zones.

The Vietnamese Amerasian story illustrates what it is like to grow up as a child of mixed race among the enemies of one's father. Abandoned for many years by the U.S. government and left to the none-too-tender mercies of the victorious Communists, Amerasians and their families often suffered very difficult lives. The stories of how they adapted to life in impoverished postwar Vietnam are sad, sometimes tragic, and occasionally creative. This book is dedicated to making Amerasians more widely known to the American public and to the wider world community—to those who have forgotten them and to those who never knew of their existence. Using Amerasians' own life histories and the results of contemporary research, I describe the ways in which these downtrodden people, discriminated against for the historical accident of their birth and mixed race, learned to cope with complex, painful circumstances in both Vietnam and the United States. While unique in certain respects, the Amerasian story has many universal themes: the neglect of the human by-products of war, the destructiveness of prejudice and racism, the impact of losing one's mother and father, the pain of abandonment, and the horrors of life amidst grinding poverty. There are undoubtedly many other child victims of war throughout the world whose stories parallel those of the Vietnamese Amerasians. By watching Amerasians' lives unfold and experiencing the ways in which they have coped with adversity, we can

---

1. United States General Accounting Office, *Vietnamese Amerasian Resettlement: Education, Employment, and Family Outcomes in the United States* (Washington, D.C.: United States General Accounting Office, 1994).

learn more about the importance of preventing such tragedies in the future and, when they cannot be prevented, about the need to come quickly to the aid of their victims.

Sitting in a resettlement "cluster site" in the South Bronx, a young Vietnamese Amerasian talked with me of his frustrations and disappointments here in the land of his father, an unknown American GI. "In Vietnam, we saw pictures of the United States. There were pretty white houses on clean, tree-lined streets. It looked like a land of dreams. I flew from Ho Chi Minh City to the Philippines, struggled to learn English, and then came here. From the time I landed at Kennedy Airport, I have seen no pretty white houses or clean, green streets— only this, the South Bronx. I live with three other Amerasians in a small, dirty apartment. All day long we listen to music, drink beer, and talk of home. We can't find jobs because we speak English so poorly. We're afraid to walk around because it's so dangerous. I wish I had known what it would be like when I was still in Vietnam. Maybe I wouldn't have come."

Was the Vietnamese Amerasian migration to the United States a tragedy of shattered expectations and broken dreams? Was the Amerasian Resettlement Program merely a guilt offering for the havoc wreaked on Vietnam and its people by the United States during the Vietnam War, a token gesture, "too little and too late," for these now grown-up children? Or was the decision to permit Amerasians and their families to immigrate to the United States a wise and humane one, offering a better life to people who in Vietnam were often no more than "the dust of life"?[2]

And what of those Amerasians unable or unwilling to leave Vietnam? Now that media and public interest in them has waned and the

2. "Dust of life" (*bui doi*) is a Vietnamese expression referring to the poorest of the poor, not only to Amerasians.

Amerasian Homecoming Program is coming to an end, these American children have returned, often with their own children, to remote villages, provincial towns, and the streets of the former Saigon. They have been forgotten and abandoned once more.

I met Kim during the final hour of my last visit to the Amerasian Transit Center in Ho Chi Minh City. She said she was thirty-seven, but looked older. Her long dark hair was tinted blond and she wore make-up to accentuate her Caucasian features. Dressed in casual Vietnamese attire—long pants, a simple flowered shirt, and plastic sandals—Kim kept insisting that I speak with her, even though I had told her several times that my schedule was full. During interviews with other Amerasians, she sat on her haunches in the adjoining patio, peering through the window and trying to catch my eye. The Transit Center staff had told me they did not believe she was Amerasian at all, but the child of a French soldier, left behind from that earlier war. This, and her dogged persistence, gradually began to annoy me, and I resolved not to meet with her. Finally however, as I gathered my belongings to leave, Kim begged to speak with me, and I reluctantly agreed.

She sat across the table and tearfully told a disjointed story that I found heart-rending. Her father, she said, was an American serviceman about whom she knew nothing. She grew up in a village in the north of the former South Vietnam, living alone with her mother, who had been cast out by her family after her affair with an American. Her mother's poverty, and her need for Kim's help around the house and garden, made it impossible for Kim to attend school; her fair skin, round eyes, and high-bridged nose made her the object of taunting and derision. She had no friends and lived a lonely, isolated life with only her mother's company. However, when news of the Amerasian Resettlement Program reached the village, Kim's status suddenly changed. She was now very much in demand, and women with bachelor sons approached her mother to see if a marriage might be arranged. Kim's rapid passage from obscurity and ostracism to popularity was due to the villagers' belief that whoever married her, an Amerasian, would earn for himself and his family a "golden passport" out of Vietnam to the unimaginable wealth of the United States. After careful consideration, she and her mother selected as her fiancé a handsome young man, much younger than she, the son of a prosperous family in the village. After the couple's wedding, Kim moved into the home of her husband's family, where she was treated with kindness and respect. The family helped Kim make application to the Amerasian Resettlement Program, paid the customary bribes, and waited. Over the course of the next year, Kim's mother became ill and died, and, although Kim missed her greatly, her husband's family provided solace and support. Eventually a letter arrived inviting Kim and her in-laws to make the long journey south to Ho Chi Minh City and the Amerasian Transit Center. There, after weeks of waiting, Kim and her husband's family were finally interviewed by U.S. officials. These all-powerful individuals were charged with determining who was and was not a "true" Amerasian; which "relatives" were "real" and which "fake"; and who, ultimately, would be granted permission to immigrate to the United States.

In the early days of the Amerasian Resettlement Program, the acceptance rate of Amerasians and their family members was high, approaching 90 percent. Few Amerasians could document their identity. Many had been born illegitimately, and their births were often not recorded in the official birth registry. After the Communist takeover of South Vietnam in April 1975, their mothers, fearing reprisal, often hid or destroyed letters and photographs linking them to the Americans. Thus, the only proof most Amerasians could offer of a connection to the United States was their mixed racial features, the color of their hair and skin or the shape of their eyes and noses. Their family relationships were equally difficult to document. This prompted many unrelated Vietnamese to pay Amerasians to claim them as family members, making them also eligible for resettlement in the United States. Gradually, however, as tales of "fake" Amerasians and unrelated "families" began to emerge and become widespread, U.S. officials grew increasingly suspicious of anyone claiming to be an Amerasian or an Amerasian's relative. As one interviewer told me over breakfast at the Majestic Hotel, "every Amerasian case is fraud until proven otherwise." By the time Kim presented for interview, the acceptance rate into the program had fallen to between 5 and 10 percent. Only those with documentation of their Amerasian or relative status were accepted. The vast majority of applicants were turned away, including, according to Transit Center officials, many real Amerasians and their families.

Kim and her husband's family did not pass the test. With their hopes for a new life in the United States shattered, the family turned on Kim, treating her with cruelty and contempt, and abandoning her at the Transit Center when they returned home. Alone in the world, Kim had no one to approach for help. Her mother was dead, her mother's family had long ago rejected her, and now her husband's family had also cast her out. She had no future in either Vietnam or the United States, and so clung to the one thing she did have, the Amerasian Transit Center. There she lived off the kindness of Center officials, who gave her food and shelter. I met Kim in the waning days of the Transit Center's life. The Amerasian Resettlement Program was coming to an end, and few new applicants presented for interviews, discouraged by the near impossibility of acceptance. Only those with nowhere else to go stayed on at the Center, dreading the day when it, too, would be closed, and they would be cast out into the streets.

Whether or not she was Amerasian, Kim's desperation was real. She begged me to intercede on her behalf, to give her some advice on where she might turn for help. I felt immensely sad for this forlorn and hopeless woman, and impotent to assist her. I asked if she could not petition the Vietnamese government to force her husband to take her back. They were, after all, legally married. She, however, could not afford a lawyer or pay the necessary bribes to gain access to the relevant government agency. And U.S. officials had told her they would not interview her again. Despite Kim's clear Caucasian features, they, too, did not believe she was Amerasian. I turned in frustration to my interpreter, a Montagnard who had studied and trained in Australia, fought for years beside the Australians and Americans, and been rewarded for his dedication by spending over a decade after the end of the war in a "re-education" camp for former South Vietnamese officers. He shrugged and said with resignation, "what can you do? There are many people like her in Vietnam. They have no one to help them, nowhere to go, and no way to make a living. It's a problem with no solution."

The Amerasian story played out against the backdrop of Vietnam's tragedy during the latter years of the war and after Saigon's fall in 1975. Postwar Vietnam, especially during the 1980s and the early 1990s, was desperately poor. All of its citizens, except for a few members of the Communist elite, were undernourished and constantly worried about their survival. As a Vietnamese woman at the Amerasian Transit Center told me, "in the years when Amerasians had to eat manioc because there was not enough rice, I, too, was eating manioc. The difference was that, in addition, I was usually able to get some fresh vegetables, and once in a while I did have rice. We were all poor, but they were poorer than most."

In addition to poverty, Amerasians also experienced prejudice and discrimination. Here, too, they were not alone. Ethnic Chinese suffered greatly in the years following the Communist takeover, especially when Vietnam went to war with China. Thousands took to the seas as boat people, and many drowned or were robbed, raped, and murdered by pirates. Vietnamese who had collaborated with the United States and its allies, the former "puppet" government of South Vietnam, were also severely treated. Many were sent off to re-education camps, often for years, or were compelled to live with their families in the harsh conditions of the New Economic Zones, remote locations in the mountains and jungles where "undesirables" were sent. Their children, like the Amerasians, were denied educational and vocational opportunities as a matter of government policy. Vietnam had been at war for decades, and there were many scores to settle.

Thus, the position of Amerasians in postwar Vietnam, while often very difficult, and at times intolerable, was not unique. Their American heritage placed them, de facto, on the losing side, and they suffered along with the rest of the vanquished. With passage of the Amerasian Homecoming Act, Amerasians gained a singular advantage—they had a place to go, a safe way to get there, and the full support of the American government. In unguarded moments, other Vietnamese immigrants to the United States, having escaped perilously as boat people or having stood in line for years waiting to be accepted into the Orderly Departure Program, have complained about the favoritism shown Amerasians. One, a waiter at a Vietnamese restaurant, said to me, "they've got it good. I fought with you guys throughout the war. All they did was get born. Then the Communists put me in a re-education camp for five years, and when I got out, they wouldn't let me get a job to support myself. I finally gave up, hopped on a boat, and sailed to Hong Kong. Many people died on that boat ride, and I was lucky to survive. Why should they get a better deal than I did?"

Vietnamese Amerasians are also not the only children of Americans scattered around present and former military bases in Asia. There are doubtless thousands of other Amerasians in Japan, Korea, Laos, the Philippines, and Thailand. However, the Amerasians of Vietnam hold a special interest for Americans. Not only are they America's children, but they were left behind in the hands of the enemies of the United States. While they have American features (whether black, Latino, or white), they behave like Vietnamese—polite and respectful of authority. Most are poorly educated and have no formal training in any vocation. Many have difficulty reading and writing Vietnamese and little knowledge of English. Those living in the countryside, where 80 percent of the Vietnamese population resides, worked for hire as agricultural laborers, planting and harvesting the rice crop. Others fished, cared for animals, gathered firewood, or worked as driver's assistants on long-distance buses and trucks. In the cities, Amerasians operated small curbside businesses, selling cigarettes and drinks or repairing bicycle tires. Others drove cyclos, the Vietnamese pedicabs which function as taxis and small goods carriers, assisted at construction sites, cleaned houses, collected garbage, or worked at other menial jobs most people would avoid. Some became beggars, trying to earn a living from the growing number of Western tourists visiting Ho Chi Minh City. A few had better luck, completing high school and going on to learn a trade such as tile laying or brick making.

Hardly any Amerasians acquired the skills—educational, linguistic or vocational—that would allow them to compete in the highly technological job market of the United States. Had the Amerasian Resettlement Program begun during or shortly after the end of the Vietnam War, Amerasians would have come to the United States at an age when they could have benefited from the many educational and vocational opportunities available here. They would have learned to speak, read, and write English fluently and would have been better able to adapt and acculturate to American life. However, the politics of the day made this impossible. Vietnam was the victorious foe, and no politician was prepared to do anything that might appear to be aiding and abetting the enemy. For years, in fact, the U.S. government argued that Amerasians were Vietnam's responsibility and took no interest in what became of them. Now they live in the United States as adults, some broken, most survivors of a life so impoverished and deprived that those of us living in comfortable surroundings can scarcely imagine its hardships. Where are they to find a place in American society, if not in the hearts of its people?

Tuan is a twenty-eight-year-old black Amerasian male, very sturdily built, and much taller than most Vietnamese. If one were to meet him on the streets of Detroit or Los Angeles, one would think he was African American. His comportment, however, is that of the rural Vietnamese. He is gently deferential, and folds his hands together and bows on meeting. He talks in soft, unassertive tones. As we spoke, the warmth of his personality gradually emerged, and he began to talk volubly and with self-deprecating humor of his past life.

Tuan's mother met his father, a black American, at the U.S. air base where she worked as a cook and he as a mess sergeant. She was already married to a Vietnamese, had ten children by him, and needed money to help her family survive. After she became pregnant with Tuan, the American sergeant gave her enough money to build two houses, one for herself and Tuan, and one for her Vietnamese husband and the other children. According to Tuan, his Vietnamese stepfather accepted his wife's relationship with the American and loved Tuan like his own child. When the American returned to the United States in 1972, he asked Tuan and his mother to accompany him. She, however, refused to go because of her other children. They never heard from him again. Tuan's mother preserved many of his father's letters and photographs, but when Vietnam was "liberated" by the Communists in 1975, she destroyed them.

Tuan grew up in a small seacoast town northeast of Saigon. He described his childhood as happy, although his schoolmates teased him so mercilessly about his dark skin that he had to drop out of school in the first grade. What made his life bearable was the love of his Vietnamese stepfather. "My stepfather loved me more than he loved my brothers and sisters. I was fatherless, and he knew he had to take the place of my father. When I grew up, I went to work and helped him support the family. I took better care of him than any of my brothers and sisters did."

After leaving school, Tuan worked around the house and garden helping his parents with the day-to-day tasks of supporting their large family. When he was fourteen he got a job looking after several other families' oxen. There were about twenty oxen in all, and Tuan would rise each morning at seven to take them out to a pasture near his home. The oxen would graze while he played with friends, napped, or cooked his lunch. After three years of this, Tuan was asked to assume responsibility for a herd of about seventy goats. Although the goats were much more difficult to oversee, he preferred them to the oxen "because I knew how to care for them. Goats have many problems, especially skin diseases and injuries to their legs. When they were crippled, I knew how to help them."

According to Tuan, the problem with herding goats is that they are unruly, easily startled, and fast, unlike the passive oxen. Goats eat leaves rather than grass, so he did not have the luxury of simply turning them out to pasture and relaxing with his friends. Instead, he had to move the herd around the outskirts of the town, constantly searching for fresh trees and bushes. The most challenging times were when it rained. "Goats are afraid of rain, so when it rains they run away in all directions seeking shelter, often running into people's houses and frightening them. It usually rains in the late afternoon. That was the time when I was herding the goats back through the town, and also the time when most families were eating dinner. The rains would come and the goats would run off every which way, often rushing into people's houses and making a mess of their dinner. Naturally they'd get angry and I'd have to apologize. I'd explain to them what goats are like and eventually they'd start laughing. Of course they'd also have to cook another dinner."

Asked if he had ever been discriminated against for being Amerasian, Tuan replied, "yes, a lot. People would say, 'you're Amerasian, why don't you go back to America?' I dealt with my feelings by working hard at jobs in which I didn't have to spend much time with other people, even my family." When I asked if he was married, Tuan said he was not. "Vietnamese girls don't like me because of my skin color. They say, 'you're too black.'" At this point Kim's common-law spouse, a white Amerasian girl who sat behind him throughout the interview, exclaimed, "he's black, but he's charming." I asked the couple why they had not married. Tuan replied, "she's beautiful, more beautiful than any other girl I've known. We want to get married, but if we do, it may complicate our application. She applied previously

13

with a fake family, was turned down, and lost her papers. If I applied with her now, the fact that we've only been together for nine months might make it look like this relationship, too, is fake." If accepted into the Amerasian Resettlement Program, Tuan will have to leave behind not only his common-law spouse but also his stepfather and family. His mother died in 1992, and his stepfather is now sixty-nine, ill and infirm, and living with one of Tuan's stepsisters. "She's busy working, so one of her children, my ten-year-old niece, looks after him. She doesn't do a very good job. I hope I can earn enough money in the U.S. to make his life in Vietnam a little easier."

What will a twenty-eight-year-old former goatherd without formal education, who speaks no English, is illiterate in Vietnamese, and has no family to rely on, do in the United States? He hopes to meet his biological father but doesn't even know his name and will, like almost all other Amerasians, probably never find him. And if he were to locate his father, what then? Would this fifty- or sixty-year-old man, probably married and with other children, welcome this now adult child of his youth, not seen or heard from in over twenty-five years? Tuan also hopes that being with people of the same skin color will make life easier. Perhaps it will, but skin color is about the only thing Tuan will have in common with most African Americans. He will not be able to communicate with them and will have little understanding of their culture, so different from the Vietnamese culture in which he was raised. Beyond his hopes, and vague expectations that life in the United States will somehow be better, Tuan brings little, beyond a survivor's resilience, that will help him succeed. Without English, transferable vocational skills, or a social support network, Tuan's life in the United States may be as difficult, and will certainly be more lonely, than his life in Vietnam.

Much of the inspiration for this book comes from my response to the courage and determination of Amerasians like Tuan who struggled to build better lives for themselves amidst great adversity. Their efforts to cope with poverty, racism, and discrimination affected me deeply and prompted me to share their stories with others. The book is organized around themes common to the lives of many Amerasians: early maternal loss, the experience of prejudice and discrimination, coping with adversity, dealing with shattered expectations for the future, and adapting to life in the United States. Each theme is framed by a brief review of current research addressing that aspect of the Amerasian experience. Most of the story, however, is told by Amerasians themselves, recounting, through their life histories, what it has meant, and continues to mean, to be a Vietnamese Amerasian in Vietnam and the United States.

Before beginning, however, a word of caution. My knowledge of Vietnamese Amerasians is based largely on single encounters, "snapshots" of complex and varied lives. I met them at the Transit Center in Ho Chi Minh City, at the Philippine Refugee Processing Center, and at cluster sites throughout the United States. All I knew of their past and present lives was what they chose to tell me. They rarely had documentation to support their claims. The needs of the moment, their relationship with my interpreter, and their perceptions of who I was and how I might use the information obtained undoubtedly influenced what they were prepared to share.

Having interviewed hundreds of Amerasians over the past eight years, in different settings and with different interpreters, I am well aware of the effects of such contextual variables. When I first returned to Saigon in 1990 my interpreters were Vietnamese government employees from the Foreign Affairs Bureau. The Amerasians appeared quite deferential to them (if not frightened) and gave responses which seemed to me to be very cautious and circumspect. As potential immigrants to the United States they were vulnerable and anxious and did not want to say anything that might compromise their immigration status. Although I attempted to make clear my role as an independent researcher, I believe that many thought I must somehow represent the

U.S. government and would be able to affect their departure. In addition, I was a Vietnam veteran of the same vintage as their fathers and often experienced what I perceived as a respectful paternal transference. Around the camp many even referred to me as "father" (*Ba*), and one went so far as to suggest to American officials in the United States that I *was* his father!

Four months later, in the relative safety of the Philippines, the Amerasians I re-interviewed seemed much more candid and relaxed. By then they knew and trusted me a little more, had escaped from Vietnam, and were assisted in their interviews by a friendly, unthreatening young college student, an ethnic Chinese Vietnamese who had escaped to the United States as a boat person. A year or two later, when I reestablished contact with some of them by telephone in the United States, they responded to me like a long-lost friend or relative to whom they eagerly poured out their hearts.

Over the seven years of my association with Transit Center officials in Ho Chi Minh City, I developed a close working relationship with Mrs. Lien Tam, the Center's Associate Director. She treated the Amerasians in a kindly and supportive manner and was trusted by them. From 1993 onward, she served as my principal interpreter in Vietnam. The ease and comfort of her relationship both with me and with the Amerasians there resulted in interviews of far greater depth and candor than those of 1990. Most of the interviews of Amerasians in Vietnam that appear in this book were conducted with her assistance, and, as a result, I have great confidence in their veracity. Even so, however, there were still important contextual variables affecting these later interviews. The most powerful was the shadow that had fallen over the Resettlement Program, resulting in a high percentage of rejections of Amerasian applicants and their families. The Amerasians were frantic to escape Vietnam before the door to the United States closed forever, and many seemed to see me as their last chance to convey a plea for help to the American people. The desperation of their situation had a powerful effect on me, and the strong emotions all of us experienced during the interview process undoubtedly influenced how they and I told their stories.

What I have recorded here are essentially verbatim transcripts of Amerasians' life histories. While I have edited them for meaning, I have not attempted to distinguish truth from fiction. However, I believe that most of what I was told is true. Individual details may have been modified, distorted, or omitted, consciously or unconsciously, but the overall picture of Amerasian life that emerged from each telling of the story seemed to me remarkably consistent.

AMERASIANS
IN VIETNAM

2 / Growing Up
without a Mother or Father

MOST VIETNAMESE AMERASIANS WERE ABANDONED BY THEIR
American fathers. Many were also abandoned by their Vietnamese
mothers and subsequent caretakers. Research on Amerasians suggests
that those who remained with their mothers had better psychological
outcomes than those raised by surrogate caretakers such as foster mothers.[1] Those with stable, continuous surrogates, on the other hand, did
better psychologically than those raised by either a succession of caretakers or by no one at all.

Oanh, a twenty-five-year-old black Amerasian girl, was born in
the Central Highlands of Vietnam. The region is a series of
inland mountains and plateaus running south along Vietnam's border
with Cambodia and Laos, adjacent to the old Ho Chi Minh Trail. Its
location made it the site of several major land battles during the Vietnam War, and many American troops were stationed there.

Oanh never knew her mother, who abandoned her at birth, but
she does have a picture of her. She also has a picture of the black
American soldier who was her father. Oanh learned about her parents

---

1. Robert S. McKelvey and John A. Webb, "Long-Term Effects of Maternal Loss
on Vietnamese Amerasians," *Journal of the American Academy of Child and Adolescent
Psychiatry* 32 (1993):1013–18.

from an unrelated Vietnamese woman, her "foster grandmother," who raised her from birth. According to her foster grandmother, Oanh's mother came from a very poor family in the region and took a job at a nearby American base to help make ends meet. There she met Oanh's father, fell in love, and became pregnant with Oanh. When her family learned of the pregnancy, they cast her out and cut off all contact. The American soldier helped support her, but had to return home before Oanh's birth. For reasons that are unclear to Oanh, her father was unable to take her mother home with him. After his departure, Oanh's mother received one letter from him, then never heard from him again. Overwhelmed by the loss of her family and her American lover, and faced with the prospect of raising a child alone, Oanh's mother became very depressed. It was during this crisis in her life that she met the woman who became Oanh's foster grandmother. The two became friends, and the foster grandmother, pitying Oanh's mother, took her in. Oanh's mother remained with the foster grandmother until Oanh's birth, then left without saying where she was going.

Aside from the photos of her mother and father, Oanh's only other connections to her parents are a childhood friend of her mother's and the remnants of the U.S. base where her father and mother met. The friend came from her mother's home village and was the only person to maintain contact with her during her pregnancy. After her mother's departure, the friend continued to visit Oanh, functioning like a surrogate family member for the abandoned girl. When Oanh was twenty, the woman told her that her mother was living in Ho Chi Minh City and gave an address where she might be found. Oanh made the long journey south by bus, but when she arrived at the apartment building, she was told by neighbors that her mother had left several months previously, leaving no forwarding address.

The military base where Oanh's father served was located only a few miles from her foster grandmother's home. Oanh often visited there, scavenging scrap metal left behind by the Americans after their departure from Vietnam. The picture of her father shows him standing in front of the base wearing his uniform. She has often visited the spot, gazing at the remnants of the base and wondering what kind of man he was.

Oanh's foster grandmother, who was in her early forties when Oanh was born, had been married, but her husband died before they could have children. Her only other living relative, a sister, was a Buddhist nun and also childless. As a result, Oanh was the only child in the family, and her foster grandmother "came to love me like her own grandchild." The two of them lived on a small farm, working the land alone and harvesting a meager crop of rice and potatoes.

As she grew older, Oanh began to realize that she was different from other people. Neighbors and schoolmates pointed at her and said she was the child of an American. She felt insulted and denied it, saying she was Vietnamese. However, "one day I looked in the mirror and noticed that my skin was much darker than everyone else's. I asked my foster grandmother if it was true that my father was American. She confirmed that it was, told me the story of my parent's relationship, and showed me the picture of my father. I felt angry, not only because I was different, but because my father had not taken responsibility for me." The taunting of her classmates, who called her "a black Amerasian" (*My den*), gradually wore down Oanh's self-confidence and, combined with her foster grandmother's poverty, caused her to drop out of school in the fifth grade.

In subsequent chapters we will see that vicious teasing was a common experience of Amerasians. It appears to have had a quality much different from that of the teasing which is a common feature of schoolyards, and it frequently led to Amerasians quitting school. Amerasians were not just different in appearance; they were children of "the enemy." Almost everyone in Vietnam had lost someone close to them during the years of the war, and especially for those who were Communists, the Americans were seen as responsible. The U.S. trade embargo, which continued into the early 1990s, was another powerful reason for anti-American sentiment and, in strongly Communist areas, deep hatred for Americans. Despite their innocence, Amerasians became scapegoats for these feelings and often experienced merciless and relentless taunting from adults and children alike.

When Oanh was twelve, her foster grandmother became gravely ill. "She knew she was dying. One day she told me she would soon die, and that if anyone were to treat me kindly, I should ask for his help." A few months later, her foster grandmother was dead and Oanh was alone in the world. Having nowhere else to turn, she stayed on at the farm for the next two years. She became increasingly withdrawn, stopped working the fields, and supported herself on what she could raise in the garden supplemented by some money left behind by her foster grandmother. Reflecting on this period in her life, Oanh said, "I was very sad, but I tried to do the things my grandmother had taught me. Fortunately I had enough to eat, but I had no friends or other company."

One day a farmer from a nearby village came to the farm and asked Oanh if she would like to live with him and his family and be their foster child. Oanh did not know the man, but thought he might be the son of one of her neighbors. "I told him to give me a month to think about it. I was very sad at the thought of leaving, because it meant I would have to leave my grandmother's grave with no one to care for it." In tears, Oanh continued, "but I had to accept his offer. I couldn't keep living by myself."

Oanh's new life with the man and his family was less like that of a foster child than that of a servant. By day she worked for hire on a nearby coffee plantation, and by night she helped care for the home and the couple's six children. While Oanh worked at the plantation, the other children went to school. "Life was very difficult. My foster mother loved her own children more than me. When I wanted something, I asked my foster father, not her. He was kind to me. I had no mother or father, had lost the only person I was close to, and was alone in the world. He loved me for my loneliness."

The paternal love of older Vietnamese men for their Amerasian step- or foster children and grandchildren is a recurring theme in the lives of Amerasians. While there are certainly examples of cruel and abusive stepfathers, many seem to have developed an especially tender and caring relationship with their Amerasian children. Perhaps there is an explanation within Vietnamese cultural tradition for this phenomenon, in which the helplessness and loneliness of Amerasians touched a responsive chord in the hearts of these men. On the other hand, it may reflect a more universal characteristic of the aging process. As George Vaillant has suggested in his book *Adaptation to Life,* male ego defense mechanisms often mature with age, evolving to a higher, more humanistic level.[2]

When she was twenty-one, Oanh met a young martial arts instructor from Ho Chi Minh City. He had come to her village to teach at a local karate club. They fell in love, and the young man asked Oanh's foster parents if they might marry. Her foster mother was against the match. She was afraid Oanh's marriage would mean the rest of the family would not be accepted into the Amerasian Resettlement Program. Her foster father, however, advised Oanh to marry her boyfriend. "He said that having a husband would make me happy. If I remained with the family, my life would not improve." Oanh took her foster father's advice, married the young martial arts instructor, and traveled south with him to Ho Chi Minh City and the Amerasian Transit Center.

Oanh's new husband proved to be loving and supportive. During the discussions with her foster family about their marriage, he advised her to deal respectfully with both parents. "He said it would be better to delay our marriage than risk breaking off relationships with them." Oanh quickly became pregnant, but lost the baby after a few months. Again, her husband provided comfort and support, and they continued to try to have a child.

2. George E. Vallant, *Adaptation to Life* (Boston: Little, Brown, 1977).

At the Amerasian Transit Center, the young couple faced a new, potentially overwhelming challenge. Oanh was accepted for the Resettlement Program, but her husband was not. "Before the interview they made us swear an oath to tell the truth. Then they separated us, asked us where and when we had met, who our friends were, and many questions about our families. We told the truth and gave the same answers. I thought the American lady would accept him, but at the end of the interview the interpreter said something to her and she gave him a rejection letter." At this point, Oanh began to cry. "Why won't they let me go to my fatherland? I am Amerasian, but now that they have rejected my husband, I have no choice but to stay here. Is there any way you can help us? Can you raise a voice for the Amerasians of Vietnam? We are fatherless. If we said something wrong in the interview it's because we are confused about our past lives. Please ask the Americans to be generous and accept us. We are victims of the war. We've lost many things. We have no father, no mother, and no relatives. How can they turn us away?"

Upset by my interview with Oanh, I went to the associate director of the Transit Center and asked if she knew why the husband had been rejected? She replied, "Oanh is definitely Amerasian. However, I think the interviewer may have suspected that the marriage was fake. Oanh's husband is tall, handsome, and intelligent. She is a simple, poorly educated village girl, and not especially attractive. Why would he marry her when he could have anyone he wanted?"

Multiple losses, poverty, and dark skin conspired to make Oanh's life difficult and her opportunities limited. Being Amerasian helped her find a handsome husband, but one wonders how long he will stay with her if they cannot emigrate to the United States.

The following story, while similar in some respects, offers a number of contrasts. Like Oanh, Trang experienced maternal loss and grinding poverty, but he was more successful at climbing Vietnam's educational and vocational ladder. Unfortunately, being Amerasian severely limited his ascent.

Trang, a twenty-nine-year-old white Amerasian, was born in a coastal city, famous for its beautiful harbor and beaches. Like Oanh, he was abandoned by his mother at birth and raised by foster parents. He knows nothing of his Vietnamese birth mother or American father. Prior to the "liberation" of Vietnam in 1975, Trang's foster parents ran a make-shift orphanage, caring for many Amerasians. His foster father was a policeman, and the income from the orphanage helped supplement his salary. Trang looks back on his years in the seacoast town as the happiest of his life. Compared to the poverty of the postwar years, the family had a high standard of living. He remembers plentiful food, attractive clothing, and a school bus that came each morning to take him to a private school. Trang was a good student, but was teased by some of his classmates, who sang a rhyming chant beginning "Amerasians have twelve ass holes." The teasing made Trang furious, and he fought back, frequently having to run home to escape a group pummeling. His foster mother told him to stop fighting and ignore the teasing. She was concerned that if he hurt the other kids, she would have to pay their doctor bills.

On April 30, 1975, Saigon fell to the North Vietnamese Army and Trang's world turned upside down. As an official of the former "puppet government," his foster father was arrested. His foster mother had to close the orphanage, returning all Amerasians to their biological mothers, and placing the five whose mothers could not be found with childless foster families. Trang was treated differently from the rest. "My foster mother loved me very much. Even though she had two children of her own, she decided to keep me." After his foster father was released from prison in 1976, the family returned to his home village in the Mekong River delta. This fertile region, the "rice bowl" of Vietnam, offered the prospect of food and work to the now disgraced former policeman.

The family had lived with his foster father's parents for only a few months when a new crisis developed. Two policemen arrived and "suggested" that Trang's foster parents leave the village and resettle in one of Vietnam's "New Economic Zones." Whether it was his foster father's connection with the old regime or Trang's Amerasian status that led to this internal exile is unclear. Either would have been a sufficient cause.

Even more upsetting for Trang was his foster father's subsequent decision to abandon his wife and children, sending them to the New Economic Zone while he remained in the village with his parents. His foster father's mother had accused his foster mother of having an affair with an American; how else could she have an Amerasian child? His foster father knew this was not true—he had helped run the orphanage—but he did not contradict his mother, accepting her demand that he cast out his "unfaithful" wife. "My foster father is ethnic Chinese, and he was the only son. A Chinese child must obey his parents, even more so than a Vietnamese child, and a Chinese mother has a lot of power over her oldest son. My foster father married my foster mother without his mother's permission. I remember them fighting a lot when I was younger. Maybe he didn't really love my foster mother and used his mother's complaints as an excuse to get rid of her." Whatever the reason, his foster mother, her two children, and Trang were compelled to leave the comforts of home and the prosperous village to travel up the Mekong River toward the Cambodian border and the wilds of the New Economic Zone.

"When we arrived there the government gave us a four-by-eight-meter thatch hut, some rice, and a bamboo boat. It was a miserable place. Mosquitoes and lice covered us. The land was uncultivated, and we had to work very hard planting and caring for our crop. There was never enough to eat. To survive we caught fish and took leftover sweet potatoes from our neighbors' fields. The neighbors would see me gathering sweet potatoes and say, 'you're American; why don't you go back to the United States instead of stealing our potatoes?'"

Trang's neighbors in the New Economic Zone were of two types. The natives, who abused him for being Amerasian, were staunch Communists and hated everything and everyone associated with the old

Saigon regime and the Americans. The others, however, were former soldiers of the Army of the Republic of Vietnam who, like Trang's family, had been exiled to the New Economic Zone after the war. These people liked him and treated him kindly. He remembers Mr B., a tank driver; Uncle S., a special forces officer; and Uncle U., commander of a construction brigade.

Once the family had established themselves and begun to eke out a meager existence, Trang was able to resume his schooling. Each morning he rose early and rowed his boat four miles down river to attend the local school. There he was teased viciously by some of his classmates, who again recited the insulting, rhyming chant of "Amerasians have twelve ass holes" and told him he should go back to America. "The teasing made me angry. I wanted to fight the students who teased me, but I knew if I did things would only get worse. Fortunately it was only a small group of children from 'political' families who teased me. Most of the other kids, and all my teachers, treated me well."

After school, Trang rowed back home and worked in his neighbors' fields for hire. When the work day was over, he got in his boat and went fishing to supplement his family's diet. When the fishing was good it was easy and fun, but there were days when he would have to fish until one or two in the morning to catch enough. "Life was very difficult. We didn't have enough food or clothing, and when we got sick we couldn't afford to buy medicine. Over time things improved, but it was a miserable life."

After graduating from high school near the top of his class, Trang applied to university, but was turned down because he was Amerasian. His only alternative was to enter a vocational training center, where he learned to be a bricklayer. Jobs were scarce, and he remained unemployed for several months after completing the course, finally finding a place with a local construction company. His time there was brief, for he soon received orders to join a youth labor force. Payment of a small bribe allowed him to enlist, instead, in the Vietnamese People's Army, the army that had fought against his American father. After training he was sent to Cambodia, where Vietnamese troops were fighting Pol Pot, the Khmer Rouge leader responsible for the Killing Fields. Trang was a good soldier, and because he was intelligent he was selected to attend officer candidate school. Unfortunately the school's political officer soon discovered that Trang was not only Amerasian, but the foster son of a former Saigon policeman. As a result he was dismissed from the school and sent back to fight in the Cambodian jungle.

After three years' service with the army, Trang was discharged and returned home to the New Economic Zone. His military experience helped gain him a job as a village policeman, a position he held for the next two years. He liked the work. It was much easier than farming or soldiering, and offered him the opportunity to get to know everyone in the area. He soon fell in love with a local girl. He was attracted to her because "she cared well for her family, worked hard, and was frugal." After seven years of marriage and two young children, he still loves her deeply. "She makes me very happy. We share everything with each other, and even when we were poor she never complained."

In 1993 Trang learned of the Amerasian Resettlement Program and decided to travel with his wife to Ho Chi Minh City to apply. He did not tell the interviewers of his service in the Vietnamese army, fearing that might disqualify him. For reasons he still does not understand, his application was rejected.

Trang and his family continue to live at the Amerasian Transit Center, hoping against hope that American officials will change their minds and accept them. In the meantime, Trang has taken a job as a bricklayer at the amusement park across the street. Asked what he will do if he is not accepted, Trang replied, "I'll do my best to get some money so I can buy a piece of land and build a house. I'd like to live here in Ho Chi Minh City, but if I can't afford it, we'll move somewhere nearby."

Despite repeated disappointments, Trang seemed an emotionally sturdy young man with a great deal of self-confidence. This may reflect his good fortune at having a foster mother who remained with him throughout his childhood. The next Amerasian was not so fortunate. Although outwardly self-confident, her mother's repeated abandonments left her with what seemed to me a very fragile and vulnerable personality.

H uong is a twenty-seven-year-old white Amerasian, the common-law spouse of the black Amerasian goatherd described in chapter 1. She was born in Ho Chi Minh City, where her mother lived with her husband, a South Vietnamese paratrooper by whom she had four children. In 1967 her mother took a job as a cook at a U.S. Army installation near Saigon. Her husband was frequently absent on maneuvers, and she soon began an affair with an American she met at the base. Huong knows nothing about him. After Huong's birth, her mother's husband learned she had given birth to an Amerasian child and came home to confront her. On the way back, however, his car crashed into a gas truck and he was killed. After his death, her mother moved with Huong and her four Vietnamese children to a coastal city, where she took a job on another U.S. base, had an affair with another American, and gave birth to a second Amerasian child, this time a boy. Unable or unwilling to care for her two Amerasian children, she left the two-year-old Huong and her newborn brother at an orphanage operated by an order of nuns. She then moved further north and took a job at a third American base. Huong did not see her again for many years.

Huong and her Amerasian half brother lived in the orphanage for the next ten years. She described her time there with humor and a touch of nostalgia. "There were too many of us for the nuns to keep an eye on all the time. So I got into a lot of mischief. One of my favorite tricks was to climb out over the orphanage gate after dinner with four or five friends. We'd gotten to know some young guys in town who taught us a little scam. They'd give us an empty ice cream crate and we'd sit by the curb crying and telling people our ice cream money had been stolen. Some of them felt sorry for us and gave us money. When we had enough, we'd give it to the young guys and they'd reward us by buying us a bowl of noodle soup. Then, at about nine thirty, we'd climb back over the gate into the orphanage. The nuns finally got wise to what we were doing. They noticed that I kept falling asleep in class, and so one evening they followed me into town. To put a stop to our little business, they ran barbed wire across the top of the gate, but the young guys dug a hole in the orphanage wall for us to crawl through. I soon lost interest in working the lost ice cream scam, but it was still fun to go out because the orphanage was a dull place and the streets were lively and exciting. Most of the time we'd just sit and watch the people passing by, although now and then we'd beg for money.

"When I was outside the orphanage, people would often come up to me and ask if I'd like to live with them. One day, when I was about twelve, I decided, 'why not?' I ran away and went to live with a couple who owned a farm outside of town. Their married daughter lived with them and she had two children, one two years old and the other three months. I got the job of looking after them. After a few months of this, I began to miss my Amerasian half brother back in the orphanage. I ran away from the family and went back to the orphanage, but the nuns refused to take me in. They said they'd called my mother, told her what had happened, and asked her to come get me. That scared me because I knew my mother would be angry at me for running away. So I took off again and went right back to the family I'd just left. I ended up staying there for five years, until I was seventeen. Although they were farmers, they didn't make me work in the fields or help with the cooking. All I had to do was care for the children. The family treated me pretty well. The only time they'd get angry was when I wouldn't mind the children properly. Then they'd beat me. The first few years I was there, life was pretty good, but when the war ended the economy fell apart and everybody had a hard time. By the late 1970s, we couldn't get much rice even though we were farmers. All we had to eat were sweet potatoes and manioc. During that time I lost a lot of weight and always felt tired."

When Huong was seventeen her eldest Vietnamese half brother

came to the farm to find her. He had been to see the nuns and they had told him what had happened and where she was living. At first he was not sure it was really Huong and asked to see photographs of her as a child. When she produced several photos showing the two of them together, he knew she was his sister. The couple with whom she had been living demanded that he pay them for raising her. He promised he would, but never did. Brother and sister went back to the orphanage, where the nuns confirmed her identity. He invited Huong to join the rest of the family in Ho Chi Minh City, where their mother had established a business selling noodle soup and was now earning enough so they could all live together again.

Huong went to the city with her brother and lived there for the next year, helping with the family business. Around that time the government decided to reduce the population of Ho Chi Minh City, swollen after the war by hungry people from the countryside searching for work. Those who could not prove long-term residence in the city were sent to New Economic Zones, where they were expected to support themselves by subsistence farming. As recent arrivals in the city, Huong and her family were "requested" to move to a New Economic Zone. The village to which they were sent was about sixty miles from Ho Chi Minh City and close to the seacoast. Huong made the journey with her mother, but stayed for only a couple of months. She found that she could not stand up to the rigors of rice cultivation. "I can endure hunger, I can work selling things on the street no matter how hot it gets, but I can't handle working in the fields." While her mother remained in the village, Huong took a job in Ho Chi Minh City as a waitress at a coffee house near the Foreign Affairs Bureau. The area was famous as a gathering point for Amerasians, who waited there hoping to meet a friendly American tourist and somehow secure a passage to the United States. It was the backdrop for many of the early photos of Amerasians that appeared in U.S. newspapers in the mid-1980s, awakening Americans' interest in the fate of their abandoned children.

After several years in the New Economic Zone, Huong's mother moved to a city notorious as a center for forgery and the creation of false identity papers. There she met a family who developed a keen interest in her Amerasian daughter. The family proposed that they buy Huong, help her apply for the Amerasian Resettlement Program, and travel with her to the United States. Huong's mother was desperate for cash and, one suspects, not very closely attached to Huong, and so agreed. Huong moved there from Ho Chi Minh City and lived with the family while they applied for her to the Resettlement Program, listing themselves as her "family." In 1991 they were interviewed. Huong was approved, but the family was not. Unwilling to part with their "golden passport" to the United States, the family refused to give her the documents that would have enabled her to emigrate. Instead, they demanded that she reapply with them. Huong, however, had had enough. She returned to live with her mother, who by now had established another noodle shop along Vietnam's main north-south artery, Route 1. There she remained for several years, selling noodles to hungry travelers and eventually meeting her goatherd common-law husband. They fell in love and moved to the Transit Center, applying separately for the Resettlement Program.

Asked how it had affected her to live for so many years away from her mother, Huong responded, "I'm not open with other people. Somehow I feel I'm inferior, maybe because I'm an Amerasian, maybe because I didn't have a mother to support me. Also, every time I wanted to do something, the people around me—whether it was the nuns, my mother, or my brother—would say, 'you're too young, you can't do that.' So I learned to keep things to myself, not telling anybody what I planned to do. Now, even though I love my husband, I seldom talk things over with him. Instead, if I want to do something, I just do it. It's not that I don't listen to other people's advice; I just like to make up my own mind. For example, when I wanted to work at the coffee shop near the Foreign Affairs Bureau my mother said, 'you shouldn't work there, it's a bad place and not suitable for a young girl.' I didn't argue with her, I just went and did it to see for myself what it was like. I figured, 'if I don't like it, I'll just leave.' Of, course, I didn't tell my mother what I was doing.

"Another thing about me is that I'm very sensitive and easily hurt. When people treat me badly, I fall apart. Even little, insignificant things can hurt me. Once I made friends with a girl, and for a while things seemed to be going fine. Then one day I asked her to go for a walk with me and she seemed a little hesitant. She never said anything, but from then on I didn't do things with her."

Sitting with Huong, I sensed a fragile, if superficially spunky girl, who seemed quite vulnerable and alone. It was as if she were hiding from me, afraid to take a chance with yet another person who might let her down. Despite the obvious charm and good nature of her black Amerasian common-law husband, I wondered if part of what brought them together was her low self-esteem. Here was someone even more downtrodden than she, who, with very few options himself, might be less likely to leave her than a person with better prospects.

3 / Prejudice and Discrimination

MOST AMERASIANS I INTERVIEWED IN VIETNAM AND THE United States reported experiencing extensive prejudice and discrimination in Vietnam. Traditionally, Vietnamese have strongly disapproved of their daughters marrying "outsiders." There is a Vietnamese proverb that suggests, "it is better to marry a village dog than a rich man elsewhere."[1] This disapproval of outsiders was even stronger for those consorting with people of another race or from another country. Adding to this traditional prejudice was the intense anti-Americanism of the postwar period. As noted earlier, almost everyone in Vietnam had lost a close family member during the "second war of resistance," and many saw the United States as the major villain in Vietnam's struggle to liberate itself from colonialism. After the war, the intense antipathy for Americans and those who sided with them appears to have become institutionalized. For example, although Vietnamese officials deny it, every Amerasian with whom I have spoken and many non-Amerasian Vietnamese report that the government of Vietnam forbade Amerasians and other children of "collaborators" to continue their studies beyond high school to the university level. Thus after the

1. U.S. General Accounting Office, *Vietnamese Amerasian Resettlement: Education, Employment, and Family Outcomes in the United States* (Washington, D.C.: U.S. General Accounting Office, 1994).

war, Amerasians became, both by popular sentiment and government decree, the objects of intense prejudice and discrimination, un- or under-educated, and relegated to menial jobs no one else wanted.

T u is a twenty-six-year-old white Amerasian woman from a village near a former U.S. Marine base. During the war her grandfather operated a small shop by the base's gate selling drinks and snacks to Vietnamese and American passersby. Tu's mother worked in the shop, and it was there she met Tu's father, a sergeant named Bill. Her father often stopped by the shop and became friendly with the family, sometimes taking Tu's mother's younger brother bird hunting. Tu knows very little of her mother's relationship with Bill. Apparently they lived together for a time, but after Tu's birth her mother returned home to live with her family, and Bill disappeared from her life. She never married, although she did have another child, this time by a Vietnamese man. The child, Tu's half sister, also lived in her grandfather's home along with Tu, her mother, grandfather, and two maternal uncles.

Tu's family were subsistence farmers and, although poor, usually had enough to eat. Tu attended the village school, which was only three hundred meters from her house. She liked school, but was constantly taunted by her classmates, who said things like "Amerasians should live in the pig pen." Tu's hair was brown, and the other students, whose hair was black, pulled her hair and called her names. She became so ashamed of her hair that she twice shaved it off. Upset by the constant teasing, Tu refused to attend school. Her grandfather encouraged her to go, often walking hand in hand with her to the school and telling her not to be upset by the teasing. It was all too much for Tu, however, and her grandfather finally relented and let her quit.

Tu remained at home helping care for the farm animals. She tried to stay away from people other than her family because she did not like being called names. Her grandfather loved her deeply and always treated her kindly. She knew that her mother loved her too, but she was busy farming and had little time to spend with her children. Tu had two close friends, neither of whom teased her, and together they spent time gathering firewood and looking after the farm animals. Aside from these friends and her immediate family, Tu had no other social contacts in the village, living a withdrawn and isolated life.

Her favorite task around the farm, and the one to which she devoted the most time, was caring for the family's ducks. Each year they bought fifty to one hundred ducklings, and Tu had the job of raising them for market. When they were small she kept them in a large basket, feeding them cooked rice, worms, and soft insects. As they grew larger, she took them out each morning to feed in the fields and, when they had eaten their fill, herded them into a pond she had fenced in so they could not run away. By noon the pond water became so hot she had to take them out, scooping them up with a small basket and carrying them back home. There she ate lunch, had a nap, then carried the ducks back to feed and swim all afternoon. Tu enjoyed raising the ducks, watching them get bigger and bigger and admiring their pretty, clean feathers.

When the ducks were fully grown, the best would be selected for breeding, while the remainder were taken to market. After they were sold she always felt sad, missing and pitying them and knowing she would never see them again. To comfort her, Tu's grandfather let her keep the prettiest duck for a pet. This made the lonely girl very happy.

As she got older, Tu had to leave the duck herding to her younger half sister and began helping her family cultivate the rice paddy. This was hard, backbreaking work. First they cleaned up the remnants of the last year's harvest and cleared away the grass. Then, after repairing the paddy and its dykes, they transferred the tender young rice seedlings by hand into the shallow water of the fields. Finally came the harvest, which required cutting the rice by hand with sickles, threshing and winnowing the grain, then grinding it in a stone pistil with an old-fashioned wooden mallet.

When she was nineteen, Tu and a friend went to a village festival held down along the beach. There she met her future husband, who was swimming with some friends. He asked permission to come back to the house and meet her family and after that began to visit regularly. She liked him because he was kind to her and generous to her family. His family was not pleased to have him spending time with an Amerasian girl, but "we were in love and so close that nothing could keep us apart." Their families finally agreed to let them live together in a common-law relationship because they could not afford a formal wedding. In Vietnam a girl normally moves into the house of her husband's family, but Tu and her partner were so poor they had to move back and forth between the two homes.

After a few years of marriage Tu had a baby, a blond-haired boy who looks very much like his mother. A year after his birth, Tu and her partner decided to apply for the Amerasian Resettlement Program and moved to Ho Chi Minh City, where they lived in the Transit Center while waiting for their application to be processed. At the time I met them they had been in the Center for nineteen months.

Asked how being an Amerasian had affected her life, Tu responded, "sometimes I feel very lonely. I have no father, few friends, and am not very involved in the community. I'd like to live in the U.S. because it's my father's homeland. I think our lives would be better there. I could study, get a decent job, and earn enough money to create a good life for my child. If I stay here I'll never be able to get any further education and will be useless. I hope it isn't too late to be accepted."

Like many other Amerasians, Tu bears the burdens of her disadvantaged minority status. After a lifetime of prejudice and discrimination she has little education and appears to have a very low opinion of herself and her capabilities. She cannot read or write and has no vocational skills transferable to a modern, technological society like that of the United States. And yet she is a willing, hard-working girl, who would probably perform any task, no matter how menial, to support her family. While it is hard to imagine a bright future for her anywhere, it is likely that a hard-working poor person can still earn a better living in the United States than in Vietnam. Whether or not she will have the opportunity to live in the United States was unclear when we last spoke. Although her application had not yet been turned down, the acceptance rate was running at only about 5 percent and, like other Amerasians in the Transit Center, she was beginning to lose hope.

Tuyet, a twenty-six-year-old white Amerasian woman, was born in Saigon. Her father was a high-ranking U.S. official and lived with Tuyet and her mother in a fashionable downtown hotel. According to her grandfather, her mother initially worked for her father as a maid, then became his lover and began to live with him. Tuyet has vague memories of life in the hotel with her parents. "Every evening my father would come home from work and my mother would carry me to the door to greet him. He'd sit down on the sofa and I'd climb up into his lap. I remember sitting in his lap and touching his cheek. He had red-white skin. My mother was slim, had long hair, and was rather tall. She loved me very much." Tuyet lived in the hotel with her father and mother until she was three years old. She was then sent to live with her grandparents in a suburb of Saigon, while her mother remained in the city. Her mother often visited her there, and on two or three occasions took her into town to see her father. "When I was four, I remember my mother going away for six to eight months, then returning home with a lot of money." At this point in her narrative, Tuyet began to cry. When I asked why she was crying she said, "I remember my mother coming home with the money for my grandparents. She said she had to go away again for a long time to make more money to support our family. She wanted very much to take me with her. Then she went away and I never saw or heard from her again. I have no idea where she is. I often used to ask my grandfather about her. All he'd say was that she'd had a very hard life. Then he'd begin to cry, and I didn't dare ask any more."

Tuyet does not remember much from her time at her grandparents' home. She lived with them, an uncle, and an aunt. The family worked as farmers, raising rice, corn, and vegetables. They stayed on for a few months after her mother's final departure, awaiting her return. However, with the fall of Saigon they decided to move to a town in the Mekong Delta where her grandfather's brother, her great uncle, lived. He was a farmer and offered to provide them with enough land to support themselves. The family's move to the Delta was prompted by concerns for their own and Tuyet's safety. The area where they lived was strongly pro-Communist and well known for its "revolutionary spirit." Her mother's long-term liaison with an American official, and her Amerasian child, would have made the family ready scapegoats there, and in the uncertain weeks and months following the Communist victory, it was unclear how "collaborators" would be treated.

Thinking back on her time in the Delta, Tuyet again began to cry. "My life has been filled with so much sadness, and there are some things that are just too painful to talk about. Life in the Delta was very difficult. We raised rice, corn, sweet potatoes, and green beans, but there were lots of insects and the crop was terrible. We never had enough to eat or clothes to wear. I remember my grandmother going out around the neighborhood begging for food, and all she had to wear was an old pair of trousers and a sleeveless blouse. She couldn't even afford sandals. I tried to help my grandfather as much as I could, and followed him around all day, carrying water from the canal to irrigate the fields and pulling weeds."

Tuyet also started school in the Delta, but only stayed for a couple of months. "The girls who sat next to me pulled my ears and called me *me My* ("American mother"—this was an insult deriving from French colonial times, when women who lived with the French were called *me Phap* or *me Tay,* French mother or Western mother). Tuyet told her teacher about the cruel teasing, but he took no notice, hitting her and telling her she was at fault for talking in class.

School was not the only place Tuyet experienced prejudice and discrimination. Whenever she walked along the path by her neighbor's house, the woman would point at her and start shouting, saying she was the child of a prostitute who had lived with an American and given birth to a half-breed. Then the neighbor's three children would chase after Tuyet and beat her with sticks. She grew so frightened of the woman that she stopped going out of the house alone. "I thought no one liked me, so I didn't get to know anybody who lived nearby. I just stayed at home with my family and worked."

Tuyet and her grandparents lived in the Delta for sixteen years, impoverished and isolated from the local community. Tuyet's grandparents were getting too old to continue farming and, in an attempt to improve the family's standard of living, her uncle, her mother's brother, left home to search for work. He finally found a job in a saw mill northeast of Ho Chi Minh City. Working hard, he was able to save enough money to buy his own saw mill, and sent for Tuyet and her grandparents to join him. There was a small plot of land attached to the saw mill, and Tuyet worked there with her uncle's wife to grow rice. "I worked all day in the fields and never went out socially because I was afraid people would be cruel to me as they had been in the Delta. I did get to know a couple of girls whose rice fields were next to ours. Whenever they needed an extra pair of hands I'd go help out, and eventually we became friends."

Tuyet also got to know a neighbor who owned a dressmaking shop. The woman liked Tuyet and offered to teach her to sew in exchange for washing clothes and cleaning the shop. When she decided to relocate her business to a nearby city she invited Tuyet to accompany her and continue her training as a seamstress. At first Tuyet's grandparents were reluctant to let her go, but finally relented, deciding it was important for her future. "My grandfather had recently had a stroke and was paralyzed and hated to see me go, but he said that if I learned a trade, and later got married, I'd be better able to help my husband support the family."

Tuyet moved to join the dressmaker at the beginning of 1993, when she was twenty-one years old. In the dressmaker's new shop there were six other young people working as apprentices. One was a man about her age who became interested in Tuyet and was kind to her. "All my life people have discriminated against me and treated me cruelly. Even as a young child I learned to fear people I didn't know well and always kept to myself. At the dressmaker's shop I was afraid to make friends with anyone, but he began to pay a lot of attention to me, asking why I was so sad. He took care of me, and we began to go out together. One day he told me he loved me and wanted to marry. At first I didn't believe it. I thought he was just taking advantage of me, marrying an Amerasian so he could go to the U.S. However, I gradually came to believe he was sincere. He was so tender-hearted and good. When I'd cry and tell him how sad I was to be fatherless and motherless, he'd console me. He'd say, 'everyone wants to be happy, to have a good life and a good education, but you've had a lot of bad luck. It's your sadness that makes me love you.'"

Tuyet and the young man asked her grandparents and his parents for their permission to marry and were wed in a simple ceremony at her grandparents' house at the beginning of 1994. His parents gave them some money as a wedding present, and they decided to use it to travel to Ho Chi Minh City and apply for the Amerasian Resettlement Program.

When I met them, Tuyet and her husband had been at the Transit Center for three years and had already been rejected at least once by U.S. officials. At the end of our interview Tuyet said to me, "please ask the U.S. government to change its mind about us and let us go to our fatherland. We've suffered so much over the last twenty years. I know I'm the child of an American. Every time I see an American, I wonder if he's my father. Please raise a voice for us."

Khoi came to our interview carrying her daughter, a little girl with blond hair and mixed Asian and Caucasian features. As we talked, the child sat quietly in her mother's lap, playing with a toy necklace. Khoi was born in a village in central Vietnam and lived there

43

all her life with her mother and grandparents. Asked how people in the village had treated her, Khoi began to cry. "Life there was terrible. The people had a deep hatred for the Americans. Not many kids liked to play with me; they tried to isolate me. The teachers despised me because I was Amerasian. Sometimes the kids would chase me away from school. I felt ashamed of myself and what I was. After four years, I quit school. Even then the local security agents kept interrogating my mother because she'd had an affair with an American."

Khoi got on well with her mother, who sometimes told her about her relationship with Khoi's father. "My mother's family was very poor, and when she was nineteen or twenty she had to start earning a living. She got a job as a bar girl at an American base, met my father there, and got pregnant. When he was transferred to another base, she went with him. They rented a house together. Then, one month before I was born, he disappeared, and she never heard from him again. My mother kept working at the bar. Then, when I was two, she moved back home."

The Amerasians described in this chapter, and in chapters to come, were often conceived out of wedlock or even when their mothers were already married to Vietnamese men. The strong taboos operative in traditional Vietnamese society against such relationships for women (although not necessarily for men) cause one to question the women's motivation in consenting to sexual relationships with Americans. One possibility, of course, is that they did not consent, but were raped, a not uncommon event during war.[2] Another is that they had sex for money. Compared to most Vietnamese, even the lowest ranking American serviceman was well to do, and Vietnamese women, especially from less affluent families, may have viewed young, lonely men with lots of money as an excellent business opportunity. Others may have fallen in love, developed short- or long-term relationships, and conceived children in the context of affairs or marriage. In a study of 115 Vietnamese

2. Arlene Eisen Bergman, *Women of Vietnam* (San Francisco: Peoples Press, 1974).

Amerasian mothers conducted at the Philippine Refugee Processing Center, Leong and Johnson found that only 12.5 percent of the women studied reported having been married to their Amerasian child's American father, but 81 percent had lived with him. Their relationships with the fathers had lasted varying lengths of time; from less than a year (36.5 percent) to as long as seven years (1.9 percent). Almost 64 percent had received support for their child from the father while he was still in Vietnam, and 11.4 percent had continued to receive support after his departure for the United States. Nearly 63 percent reported that they had expected to join the father after he first left Vietnam.[3] While these figures do not allow us to draw definitive conclusions about the nature and quality of the relationships existing between Vietnamese Amerasians' mothers and their American fathers, they do suggest that most were more than transitory affairs or "one-night stands."

Khoi's mother never married, living with her parents, aunts, and uncles, and working for hire as an agricultural laborer. The village where they lived was located in Vietnam's coastal plain. There were a few small hills, but most of the area was flat and given over to rice cultivation. "It was a poor, overcrowded place. The climate wasn't good for raising rice. We had no land of our own and, compared to our neighbors, our standard of living was very low. To earn extra money, I'd gather snails, clams, and herbs in the forest."

Khoi's family treated her well, but other villagers were very cruel, calling her "American girl" and telling her to go back to her fatherland. Aside from one friend, no one outside her family would play with her, and she always had to be on guard because the other children in the village liked to chase her and beat her up.

When she was eighteen Khoi and her mother went to Vietnam's

---

3. Frederick T. Leong and Mark C. Johnson, *Vietnamese Amerasian Mothers: Psychological Distress and High-Risk Factors* (Washington, D.C.: Office of Refugee Resettlement, Department of Health and Human Services, 1992).

Central Highlands to earn extra money helping with the coffee harvest. There she met her future husband, who was also helping with the harvest. "We were both in the same situation. We had miserable lives. Mine was bad because I was an Amerasian. His was bad because he was an orphan. My mother liked him, and when we fell in love she invited him to come back and live with us in the village." They lived together with the family for a couple of years, then moved to their own house. A year later the little girl now sitting on her lap was born. After marriage and the birth of her child, Khoi's life began to improve a little. The villagers stopped taunting her, although every now and then one of them would say, "why don't you go back to America?"

In 1993, when she was twenty-three years old, Khoi decided to do just that, applying for the Amerasian Resettlement Program. Her mother had died the year before, her grandparents were long dead, and there was little to hold her in the village. Moving to the Amerasian Transit Center with her husband and daughter in 1994, she was pleased to find they could earn more money in the city than back home. Even better, hardly anyone teased her anymore, except for the occasional heckler on the street who suggested that she go back to the United States.

Asked why she wanted to go to the United States, Khoi responded, "I want to go and find my father. Life here is just too terrible. We can never make enough money to support ourselves. I've met a few Amerasians who've come back from the U.S. and they've told us how much better their lives are there. I've got American blood in me, and my dream is to go back to my fatherland. My husband also thinks we'll have a better life in the U.S."

Like many other Amerasians I met at the Transit Center during my final visit in 1997, Khoi was frightened by rumors that the Resettlement Program was coming to an end and the Center was about to close. She and her husband had already been turned down once and were concerned that the door might now be closing for good. "All

Amerasians want to resettle in the United States. From the day we were born, the constant discrimination in Vietnam has made our lives awful. When we go for our ODP interviews, they keep asking for information about our fathers and for documentation. But after Liberation Day, everyone burned their papers! They were terrified about what would happen if the government knew they'd been with the Americans. Now the ODP asks us all these questions. If we get mixed up, they deny our application. I have nothing at all back in my village. My mother's house has collapsed, and my relatives there are very old and can't support us. If we're turned out of here, we'll have nowhere to go, no place to live. We'll be street people. We've suffered all our lives and we just want to get out of Vietnam."

While many Amerasians experienced prejudice and discrimination in Vietnam, black Amerasians appear to have experienced more than others. I often heard white Amerasians comment that their fair skin bestowed certain advantages on them in Vietnam, where it is considered attractive. Black Amerasians, on the other hand, have never told me their darker skin color helped them. While scientific studies differ on whether or not a father's ethnic background is a risk factor for increased levels of psychological distress among Amerasians,[4] many observers have remarked that black Amerasians seem to have experienced more than their share of difficulties. The cause of this intense discrimination is not clear. It may derive from a general Vietnamese prejudice against those with darker skin, or from past experiences with French African colonial troops, or from lessons learned from Americans during the war. The following story suggests some of the additional problems faced by black Amerasians growing up in Vietnam, and how one,

---

4. Compare Robert S. McKelvey, John A. Webb, and Alice R. Mao, "Premigratory Risk Factors in Vietnamese Amerasians," *American Journal of Psychiatry* 150 (1993): 470–73, and J. Kirk Felsman et al., *Vietnamese Amerasians: Practical Implications of Current Research* (Washington, D.C.: Office of Refugee Resettlement, Department of Health and Human Services, 1989).

at least, managed to adapt successfully to his disadvantaged minority status.

N am, who was twenty-seven when I met him, knows nothing of his biological father or mother. He was abandoned in front of a church and lived in an orphanage there until he was adopted by his foster mother. Nam's earliest memory is of being left in front of the church and of a priest dressed in a black robe and wearing a cross coming out and carrying him back inside. "I couldn't speak then; I just remember the image. I cried when he picked me up and carried me back to the church, and I can still remember when he took me inside. I saw many children my age. The priests and nuns were very generous. They raised a lot of Amerasians who'd been left in front of the church. They did it out of love for the poor and abandoned."

Nam was taken in by his foster mother when he was three or four. She was a hospital midwife from a town in the Mekong Delta and had come to the city where he lived on a tour. She visited the orphanage, saw Nam, and fell in love with him. "As a little child, I was very beautiful." At the time she took him in, Nam's foster mother was thirty years old, had a daughter four years older than Nam, and was divorced. "My foster mother had a special love for me. She usually treated me the same as her daughter, but sometimes she'd treat her better than me. When my foster sister did something wrong, she'd often blame me for it. Often my foster mother found out the truth and asked her not to behave like that, but sometimes she believed her and punished me unfairly. When she was unfair, I'd feel sad and think she didn't love me because I was adopted. But I didn't feel sad for long because I loved her very much, and besides, I can't stay mad at anyone."

His foster mother did not earn much money working as a midwife, and she had no land to farm to supplement her income. As a result, their standard of living was substantially lower than that of their neighbors, who raised and sold rice. Nam completed only a couple of years of school. He was taunted by classmates, who called him *My den* (black American) and chanted "Amerasians have twelve ass holes." He told his teachers about the name calling, but they could not stop it outside of class. "The teasing made me very sad, but it wasn't the main reason I left school. I just preferred playing, and besides, my family was poor, and it was hard for my mother to afford the school fees. Still she tried to make me continue, but I quit anyway. After I stopped, I helped out around the house carrying water and made extra money selling lottery tickets. I didn't make much money doing it, but I'd give half of what I earned to my mother and keep the rest for candy and cookies."

At the age of seventeen Nam left home. His departure was precipitated by a quarrel with his sister. Over the years they had fought about many things and, although he loved her, he was also deeply angry and resentful at the way she treated him. On the morning of the day he left she had asked him to get water from the village well, which was located three hundred meters from their house. "I was hungry, so I took a break to get something to eat. When my sister saw me, she asked why I hadn't finished getting the water. She kept on nagging me, and I got so mad I just left home. I went into town and found a bus that was heading to a town northeast of Ho Chi Minh City. I asked the driver if he'd give me a lift. He agreed, and so off I went."

Nam lived in the town for the next four years. After getting off the bus, he walked directly to a nearby house and asked the family if he could work for them. They owned a coffee and pepper plantation, needed help, and took him in. "Life there was difficult at first, but I got used to it, and it soon became routine. The husband and wife treated me well, but their children were jealous because I worked hard and was honest while they were lazy and stole from their parents. When I first arrived, people thought I was strange because of my dark skin, but eventually the older ones came to like me. Among the young, I didn't have many friends, maybe because they were too busy working, or maybe because of my skin."

During the four years he lived in the town, Nam never told his

49

mother and sister where he was. "At night I'd think about my mother all the time. I missed her and wanted to write to her, but my writing is very bad and I didn't know how to express my feelings on paper. Finally I got very homesick for her and told my boss I was going for a visit. I didn't intend to stay, but when I got there my mother wouldn't let me leave again. At first she was angry at me for having left without telling her and staying away so long, but I apologized and she forgave me."

Back home, Nam took a job as a laborer in the local rice mill. There he met his future wife. "She sold rice and had come to the mill to buy more supplies. At first she was frightened of me. She'd never seen a person with dark skin. But I was hard working and helpful, and she gradually came to like me. Her father was opposed to our getting married. He'd promised to marry her to a friend's son, but my mother-in-law persuaded him to change his mind."

Nam first heard about the Resettlement Program from Amerasian friends in 1992. Initially he planned to apply for himself and his mother, but the local authorities gave her a hard time, saying he was not her child, and would not include him on her household certificate. Also, her parents were still alive, and she felt obliged to care for them, so in the end she decided not to go. Nam applied for the program before his marriage, so his wife and child also were not included in his application. As a result, he will be going to the United States alone. "My wife trusts me and is willing to let me go on ahead. After I get there, I'll sponsor them to join me."

Asked why he wants to go to the United States, Nam responded, "all Amerasians want to go because it's their fatherland. I want to go because life in Vietnam is very difficult and I hope to have a better life there." Did he think that the lives of Amerasians in Vietnam were more difficult than those of other Vietnamese? "Other Vietnamese have relatives who can help them. I've always had to work by myself to make a living. I can't get included on my mother's household certificate, proving I live there with them, so it's as if I don't even exist."

Despite being black and experiencing the prejudice of neighbors, classmates, and workmates, Nam appeared to have a sense of his own worth and a conviction that, whatever his skin color, he was a good and lovable person. He coped with prejudice by working hard and trying to be friendly and helpful. Initially put off by his skin color, most people came to like and value him. His overall adjustment seems to have been good, and he had achieved as much as one might expect in impoverished postwar Vietnam for a person with very limited education and little family support.

4 / Adventurers and Entrepreneurs

IT IS EASY TO UNDERSTAND HOW CHILDREN LIVING IN POVERTY among fractured, unsupportive families, constantly exposed to prejudice and discrimination, and offered few educational and vocational opportunities, might grow up to be dysfunctional, unhappy, and unsuccessful adults. More difficult to understand are those children who somehow rise above their surroundings and circumstances to become successful and well adjusted. In recent years research in child development has sought to identify and understand the characteristics of children who are able to overcome adversity.[1] These adaptive traits, called protective factors, appear to promote resiliency, an innate capacity to cope successfully with potentially overwhelming problems. In contrast are risk factors, those circumstances and traits associated with later disease and disability. Despite significant adversity, most Amerasians tried to build better lives for themselves in Vietnam. They became "survivors," struggling, successfully and unsuccessfully, to overcome the many obstacles confronting them. The following stories illustrate especially interesting and colorful Amerasian adaptations to life in Vietnam.

1. Philip Graham, "Prevention," in *Child and Adolescent Psychiatry: Modern Approaches,* ed. Michael Rutter, Eric Taylor, and Lionel Hersov, 3rd ed. (London: Blackwell, 1994), 815–16.

52

S ang is a twenty-seven-year-old white Amerasian from a village in south central Vietnam. The area in which he grew up is located close to the mountains, a river, and the sea, and those who live there support themselves by cultivating rice and fishing.

Sang's mother met his American father at a PX where they both worked as civilian contractors. The only thing Sang knows about his father is that his name was Mark and he was a white American. Sang's father left Vietnam while his mother was pregnant with him, inviting her to join him in the United States. She decided not to go, however, because she was the only child of her parents still living at home and felt responsible for them. After his father's departure, Sang's mother returned to her home village, maintaining a tenuous contact with him through a mutual Vietnamese friend who was married to an American. Sang's father sent money once or twice through this friend, but after she, too, moved away, Sang and his mother lost all contact and never heard from him again.

Sang's earliest memories of childhood are from his mother's home village. There he and his mother lived with her aging parents, both of whom were too old to cultivate the fields. She had to work to support the entire family, raising rice on the family's land and selling what they did not need. She had little time to care for Sang, so parenting responsibilities fell to her parents. Although she did not spend much time with him, Sang believes his mother must have loved him; otherwise she would have remarried and had additional children. He can remember her disciplining him, spanking or yelling at him when he misbehaved. Sang also believes that his grandmother loved him very much but that, for reasons he does not understand, his grandfather did not. He noticed that his grandfather seemed to prefer Sang's cousins, giving them more money and more beautiful toys. Although this made Sang angry, he kept his feelings to himself. "If a person loves me, I'm happy. If not, I just try to accept it."

Despite their poverty, Sang's mother wanted him to continue his schooling rather than join her in the rice fields. By the time he was eight or nine, Sang had already begun to realize that his lighter skin color made him different from those around him. Schoolmates and villagers called him "Amerasian," a taunt he did not initially mind because he thought his lighter skin made him look handsome. Sang's grandmother encouraged him to ignore what people said, telling him that if he worked hard, people would treat him well. However, by the time Sang had reached eighth grade, the teasing had become unbearable. Sang's teachers also discriminated against him for being Amerasian, never praising him when he did well and noticing him only when he did something wrong. While he now recognizes that these perceptions may have been a symptom of his youth and immaturity, the conviction grew that no matter how hard he worked he would never get ahead. Finally, in despair over his prospects, Sang decided to leave school and go to work.

After a lengthy search, Sang found a job as a brick and tile maker, but six months of this tedious, poorly paid work persuaded him to try something more exciting and rewarding. Deep in the jungles of Vietnam grows a rare and exotic tree, the *cay gio,* or "wind tree." The sap of this tree is very precious and can be dried either to make incense for religious ceremonies or for use as an herbal medicine. Finer varieties of the dried sap could be sold to merchants from Hong Kong and Taiwan for as much as nine thousand U.S. dollars per kilogram.

Along with several other adventurers, Sang prepared enough food for two to three months, rode a bus to the end of the line, then walked fifteen days deep into the jungle carrying a 100-pound knapsack. Sang is not a large person, weighing only 140 pounds himself, so such a burden was considerable. In the jungle he and his companions set up camp by a stream and fanned out in all directions looking for the wind tree. It was very hard to find, and they might search for weeks without discovering one. When they did find a tree, they took 10 percent of their profits and prepared a feast to thank the gods for their success. The remainder was then divided equally among them.

Sang loved the work, both for the adventure and for the large amounts of money he could earn. Best of all were the times when they found the rarest of the rare, a special variety of sap (*ky nam huong*) for which the merchants paid a fortune. Sang's efforts to find this particular sap became ever more strenuous. He extended his range, three times making the long and difficult journey to the far north of Vietnam by the mountainous border with China where the best varieties of *cay gio* were to be found.

Despite the allure of the wind tree and its precious sap, the jungle was a dangerous place. There were bears, tigers, elephants, storms, floods, and disease. Each danger required a different approach. As Sang explained, "bears can climb trees faster than people, but not rocks. Since we could outrun the bears, we'd scamper out onto the rocks and be safe. Elephants are afraid of fire, so we kept a fire going at night by our base camp to keep them away. We were terrified of tigers, but whenever we saw them we prayed to God and the tigers ran away." Disease, however, was another matter. After several years of work in the jungle, Sang contracted malaria. He had seven or eight bouts of it, the last of which was so severe he nearly died. "They gave me oxygen in the hospital for seven days and at the end I was so sick the doctor thought I was dead. They carried me to the morgue, but later in the day I woke up, felt thirsty, and got myself a drink of water." Sang was so debilitated by the illness that his mother had to be called to come and take him home.

Sang remained in his home village for about a year, revelling in the money he had made hunting the wind tree and recovering his strength. All told, he had earned almost $1,200 dollars, a fortune in the Vietnam of the late 1980s. Unfortunately for Sang, at about this time the government of Vietnam decided they should preserve the wind tree and made its harvesting illegal. This did not deter him, and as his health returned, he sought ways to resume his profitable career. To camouflage his intentions, Sang moved with several friends to a town not far from the jungle where he began to cut timber and make charcoal. This gave him not only a source of income, but, more important, access to places where the wind tree might be found. Gradually he and his friends returned to hunting for the tree and its fragrant sap.

In the town where he worked, Sang met a young Amerasian girl, and the two fell in love. Initially the girl's mother accepted Sang as a suitor. She was impressed by all the money he had accumulated selling wind tree sap and thought his family must be rich. However, when she went to visit his mother and arrange the wedding, she saw that the family was very poor and changed her mind. An attractive, young Amerasian girl was a valuable commodity in the early 1990s, a "golden passport" out of Vietnam, and she did not want to waste her on a poor man. As Sang expressed it, "my girl friend is Amerasian, but she looks like a very small American. Many people wanted to marry her, both to have a beautiful wife and to be able to go to America."

Having learned of the Amerasian Resettlement Program from his girl friend and other friends in the town, Sang decided to go to Ho Chi Minh City and apply. Returning to his home village with the necessary paperwork, he completed and submitted it and waited for a reply. After several months of waiting, he decided to return to see his girl friend and to continue hunting for the wind tree. During his absence she, too, had applied for the Resettlement Program, and been approved. Her family, however, was rejected, and so she decided not to go. Over the next two years the young couple's love for one another deepened, despite her mother's objections. Frustrated by her refusal to let them marry, they decided to run away to Ho Chi Minh City, where they would live as common-law man and wife in the Amerasian Transit Center while awaiting his interview for the Resettlement Program.

When I met Sang and his partner they had been living in the Transit Center for almost four years. By then his wife was pregnant and Sang was working across the street at the Dam Sen amusement park caring for plants and laying bricks. At the Transit Center, Sang had maintained contact with his mother, who visited them twice, while he returned home once. His mother was soon to come and live with them, both to help care for the new baby and to be available for the interview that would decide whether or not they would all be permitted to immigrate to the United States. Sang's feelings toward his mother are ambivalent. "I love my mother very much, but I have lived apart from her for a long time. Whenever we do live together, we end up quarreling after two or three days."

Asked what he would do if he and his partner were not accepted for the Resettlement Program, Sang replied, "I hope and pray they accept us. We would have a much brighter future in the U.S. than in Vietnam. However, if we're rejected then it is God's will and we'll just have to accept it."

H ai, a twenty-six-year-old black Amerasian, was raised by a foster family in a village near Ho Chi Minh City. He knows little of his biological parents. According to his foster mother, his biological mother became sick during the first year of Hai's life and dropped him off at the foster family's home, staying with them for only one day. She left behind a shirt, some photographs, and a few documents relating to Hai's birth and identity. After the fall of Saigon, when Hai was four years old, the foster family burned most of the papers, not wanting to get into trouble with the new government for having an Amerasian child. All that remains is a photocopy of his father's dog tags and a photograph of Hai in his arms. From the photograph, Hai described his father as "brown-skinned—not real white and not real black."

The foster family consisted of a foster mother and father and their six biological children, all younger than Hai. The family earned its living running a coffee shop, and they were able to achieve a higher standard of living than most of their neighbors. Hai's primary role in the family was to care for his younger foster siblings. He carried them around and made sure they did not stay out in the sun too long. If the foster parents were not satisfied with the care he gave their children, they scolded him or withheld food. According to Hai, "my foster parents weren't cruel, but they didn't seem to care very much about me. I was just there to work and help out with the children." He got along well enough with his foster siblings, but had to work much harder than they did. Overall, life in the family was "sometimes good and sometimes bad. The way my foster parents treated me was good enough. They fed me and raised me."

Hai did not experience much discrimination growing up. People commented on his being Amerasian, but "it didn't hurt my feelings or upset me. I just tried to be friendly." He didn't have many friends, partly because he was busy, partly because he tried to avoid people with "bad behavior." "The way I like to live is to work hard, come home, clean up, and go to bed. I don't smoke or drink." He had one close friend, also an Amerasian, who did not smoke or drink and seemed to share his values: "We thought and felt the same about most things."

In addition to caring for his foster siblings, from the age of eight or nine Hai also helped out around his foster parents' coffee shop, serving drinks and selling coffee to customers. With all the work he was required to do, he was not able to continue with his studies and had to drop out of school in the second grade. He liked working in the coffee shop, but found his foster father's behavior very trying. "He was a nice guy, but he was money hungry and wanted the lion's share of everything we earned. My foster mother and I didn't like not being able to keep at least some of what we made. She and he would often quarrel about money, sometimes in front of the customers, and once in a while he'd get so mad he'd chase customers out of the shop. That wasn't very good for business."

When he was fourteen, Hai decided he had had enough of his foster father. "I got really angry with him one day and decided I'd leave for good. There was a rumor going around that you could make good money cutting down trees in the Central Highlands, so I caught a bus and went there." The place where he worked is not far from the resort city of Da Lat, where French colonial officials once vacationed to escape from the sweltering heat of Saigon. Although he knew no one there, Hai quickly found a job gathering fallen timber in the forest to be sold for firewood in town. There were a number of people doing the same thing, all living together in little huts in the forest. They got up early each morning, collected as much fallen timber as they could, and carted it off to a waiting truck that took them into town. There they spent the day selling the wood, riding back each evening to their forest homes. Hai enjoyed the work. "I liked being out of town, got paid regularly, and made enough money to support myself and even save a little."

After a couple of years working there, Hai decided it was time to return home. During the rainy season, it was cold and uncomfortable in his hut and also harder to make money because the wood was wet. "One day the road was so slippery I fell off the truck on the way into town. That scared me, and I decided to go home. I'd made good money there, saved a lot, and was able to bring $300 home with me. The money made my family very happy, and they received me warmly. So I went back to work in the family business selling coffee."

After a few months at home, however, Hai realized that nothing had changed. His foster father was as greedy and impulsive as ever, and after a few quarrels Hai decided to leave again. This time he went to join a friend in another small town near Da Lat where there was work on a coffee plantation. For the next two years he lived and worked with the planter and his family, cutting grass around the coffee plants and growing corn. He was paid a good salary and treated well by the planter because labor was in short supply. Unfortunately, Hai contracted malaria and had to be hospitalized. After two weeks he was sufficiently recovered to return to the plantation, but decided he had had enough of cold weather, fearing it would make him sick again. The plantation owner gave him a bonus for his two years of work, and he returned home again to his foster family.

This time, however, Hai had no intention of staying. A friend was engaged in smuggling cigarettes from Cambodia to Vietnam, and Hai decided he would try his luck at this dangerous, but highly remunerative, business. He and his colleagues bought "Jet" cigarettes in Cambodia, secreted them on their persons, and rode a passenger bus across the Vietnamese border, making as many as ten trips a day. If successful, each trip would net them $5, a princely sum in a country where the average wage was then about $150 a year. To avoid detection, the smugglers sneaked around the edges of the large crowds gathered at the border crossing. If caught, the guards confiscated everything and the smugglers had to pay a bribe to avoid further trouble.

Hai worked as a smuggler for almost a year, but after getting caught a number of times decided it was too nerve-racking and found an honest job working in a noodle shop on the Cambodian side of the border. Here he met many Vietnamese trying to escape to Thailand and the West. They were led by guides who helped them find a way through the Cambodian jungle to the Thai border. After six months in the noodle shop, Hai was ready for a change. He considered his options: to return to the terrors of smuggling, to revisit his quarreling foster family's coffee shop, or to endure another cold, malarial season in the forests. Finally he decided to try his luck abroad. His father was American, and Hai knew his name; maybe he could find him in the United States.

Hai's first attempt to escape was not a success. Along with fifty other Vietnamese, he boarded a truck in Cambodia and started off toward Thailand. Unfortunately, as they neared the Thai border they were apprehended by a Cambodian patrol and taken back to Vietnam. Undeterred, Hai tried again. He found a second group, and this time they were more clever, getting off the truck some distance from the border and walking for two days through the jungle. The group had a guide and some water, but only a little rice and salt to eat. Close to the border a band of robbers fell upon them. At gunpoint, they searched everyone for gold or jewelry. This was a lucrative business, for many people fleeing Vietnam converted everything they had into gold, carrying it with them on the journey West. When the robbers had taken everything of value they let the group proceed on toward Thailand. Reaching a beach, they found several small boats waiting to transport them to a larger vessel, which carried them as "boat people" to Thailand. There they were put ashore on another beach in a swampy area near the jungle. Now on their own, the refugees walked on into the jungle, where they came upon a small village. The villagers provided them with food and clothing, then promptly turned them over to the Thai authorities. They were taken to a temporary refugee camp where they remained for a month and were then shifted to a larger, more permanent camp. Here Thai immigration officers conducted interviews, trying to determine who they were, whether or not their stories made sense, and who among should be considered legitimate refugees.

In the camp, Hai was surprised to discover his foster father and one of his foster siblings! Unbeknownst to Hai, they, too, had decided to flee Vietnam to prepare the way for the rest of the family to escape. Despite his ambivalence toward his foster father, he was happy to see him, for together they stood a much better chance of surviving than those who were alone.

Hai described life in the camp as "not so bad." "If you kept out of trouble, they left you alone." People in the camp were given adequate food, clothing, and shelter, and for an ambitious person like Hai there were even opportunities to start a business. Initially he carried water from the well to the wash house, earning 20 *Baht* (approximately 80 cents) for transporting two 50-liter drums about 500 meters. Eventually he and his foster father developed a more profitable business, baking bread and selling it and ice cream to others in the camp.

Camp life, however, did have its ugly side. Everyone in the camp claimed they were boat people and thus entitled to refugee status. When their identities were verified, however, many proved to be other than legitimate refugees, and their requests for asylum were denied. People who had languished in the camp for months or years were understandably angry when told they would have to return to Vietnam, and there were many demonstrations, some of which turned violent. Hai tried to keep clear of these confrontations, focusing instead on his business. All told, Hai, his foster father, and his foster brother remained in the camp for four years. In the end their request for asylum was denied. As Vietnamese citizens, they were told that they would have to return to Vietnam and apply from there for permission to emigrate. The three were taken to an airport, given $50 each, and flown back to Ho Chi Minh City. There they were placed briefly in a temporary camp and then sent home. After they had been at home a month, a representative of the United Nations' High Commissioner for Refugees arrived and gave each of them an additional $360. Along with the $50 they had been given on the plane, they now had a total of $1,230, more than enough to reestablish the family coffee business.

Predictably, however, Hai's foster father again upset their plans. Rather than invest the money in a new business, he gambled it away. With what remained, he purchased the Vietnamese equivalent of a Cadillac—a Honda "Dream" motorbike. Hai was disgusted. He and the family had worked so hard, and suffered so much, trying to achieve a stable life, yet every time they began to get ahead his foster father's greed and extravagance messed things up. His foster mother, too, had had enough. She left her reckless husband, took the children, and established a new business in the village selling pork. Rather than join her and his foster siblings, Hai decided to try again to reach the United States, this time through the Amerasian Resettlement Program. He took a bus south to Ho Chi Minh City, presented himself at the Transit Center, and applied for permission to immigrate to the United States. When I met him three years later, Hai was still waiting for his fate to be decided by American officials. In the meantime he had gone into business for himself, this time distributing pork to nearby shops.

Hai is an ambitious, hard-working entrepreneur. Had he been able to apply his talents in a more prosperous country like the United States, who knows how far he might have gone? But Vietnam in the late 1980s and early 1990s was an impoverished, hard-scrabble place, cut off from the rest of the world by the U.S. trade embargo, and with little to offer its citizens other than a life of dreary toil.

Ket is a twenty-seven-year-old white Amerasian woman from a small rural town near Ho Chi Minh City. Prior to Ket's birth her mother had been married to a Vietnamese soldier by whom she had two children. After her husband was killed in action, she went to live with her parents, opening a small roadside coffee shop in front of their home. There she met Ket's father, Tom, a sergeant in a nearby road construction battalion, who often stopped in for a drink. He was a tall, slender young man with light brown hair. They fell in love and, because Tom was prepared to contribute money for the family's upkeep, Ket's mother's parents gave consent for them to live together. When Tom's battalion moved away to begin work on an airport, her mother left her business and two children behind and followed him. For the next two and a half years Ket's mother, and eventually Ket, went wherever Tom and the construction battalion were sent. Then Tom was transferred back to the United States. He encouraged Ket's mother to go with him, making all the arrangements for her to do so, but her mother's mother was so upset by the prospect of losing her only daughter and granddaughter that Ket's mother decided not to go. After his departure, Tom sent money and gifts for the next two or three months, then stopped writing. They never heard from him again. Aside from his first name and a vague description of his appearance, the only thing Ket knows about her father is that his sister worked in a department store selling clothes.

Following Tom's departure, Ket's mother returned with Ket to her home town, where she lived with her mother and her two sons. Initially she supported the family with the coffee shop, but after the war ended and food became scarce, she found a more lucrative business, selling contraband rice in Ho Chi Minh City. In postwar Vietnam the distribution and sale of rice was controlled by the government. It was illegal for individuals to sell rice privately. Ket's mother, however, defied the law, buying rice in her home town, where it was plentiful and cheap, and transporting it by bus for sale in the city. Ket worked with her mother, joining her on the trip into town and helping hide the rice when the police were near. They were caught a few times, but the police never did anything more than confiscate the rice. The business was so lucrative, despite its risks, that Ket's mother pulled her out of school in the second grade so she could work full time. Ket was not unhappy to leave. She had not started school until the age of nine and, like many other Amerasians, had only then come to realize she was different from other Vietnamese. Her schoolmates teased her, calling her "Amerasian" and "half-breed." Although her teachers treated her kindly and her mother told her to ignore the name calling, it was difficult for a nine year old to be the continual object of such abuse.

In business, on the other hand, Ket found that being an Amerasian offered advantages. Her fair skin made her seem very attractive in a country where light skin was valued as a sign of social privilege, connoting not having to work outside under the hot tropical sun. In Ho Chi Minh City, for example, women riding motorbikes wear not only a broad-brimmed hat, but also long gloves pulled up far above their elbows to prevent tanning.

Ket worked full time with her mother for the next two years, then decided to put her good looks and business acumen to the test by starting a business of her own. As the wife of a Saigon soldier, the mistress of an American, and the mother of an Amerasian child, Ket's mother was not in the new government's good graces. Along with other "collaborators," she was encouraged to relocate to one of the New Economic Zones. Rather than comply, Ket's mother moved her family to the Mekong Delta. There she would be away from her gossipy home town neighbors and the local police, all of whom knew her background. She would also be close to an inexhaustible supply of rice that could be purchased far more cheaply than at home.

During the time she worked with her mother smuggling rice to Ho Chi Minh City, Ket was able to save a lot of money. So when the family moved south, she established herself independently as a vendor on a ferry running across one of the Mekong Delta's many rivers. At first she sold pineapples, watermelons, and mangoes, but after earning additional money, she switched to a more profitable commodity, cigarettes smuggled from Cambodia. Ket's and her mother's trade in contraband enabled them to earn far more than the average Vietnamese, and soon they were providing the family with a very comfortable standard of living.

Selling cigarettes on the ferry brought Ket more than money, for it was here that she met her future husband. He sometimes took the ferry to visit his aunt across the river, and after a few meetings the young couple fell in love. Asked what had attracted her to him, Ket replied, "it was God's will. I don't know why I loved him. We didn't meet often, only a few times during the year before we got married. Now we've been married for seven years and have never quarreled. He's a very pleasant person and everyone likes him. He's kind to other people and easygoing." Ket's new husband was a baker, and after their marriage she was able to help him establish a profitable business baking and selling *bahn mi,* the baguettes introduced by the French that have remained a staple of the Vietnamese diet.

To her relief and delight, Ket found that her new husband's family, as well their neighbors, accepted her easily. The couple had two children, a girl born in 1992 and a boy born in 1994. Surrounded by family and friends, and established in a profitable business, Ket seemed to have a stable and secure future. And yet, when an opportunity arose to apply for the Amerasian Resettlement Program, she and her husband decided to take it. What made her want to go to the United States? "I want to find my father and give my children the opportunity for a brighter future. In the U.S. my husband and I will be able to earn more money than in Vietnam so our children can go to school and have a better life." What would she say to her father if she were to find him? "I'd ask him why he didn't write to my mother and me. We stayed behind in Vietnam and had a lot of problems. We had to work hard to make a living and our neighbors didn't like us very much because my mother had lived with an American and given birth to an Amerasian." How had being an Amerasian affected her life? "There are both good and bad things about being an Amerasian. I was teased a lot by other kids when I was a child, and that was very painful. On the other hand, my fair skin made me more beautiful than the other girls selling cigarettes on the ferry, so I was able to sell a lot more than they did."

Ket and her husband had been in the Amerasian Transit Center for two years when I first met them. Not surprisingly, this active, industrious woman had established a couple of businesses there, one selling fruit on the street running by the Center's front gate and the other a small store in her room where she sold drinks, snacks, and cigarettes to others waiting to be interviewed for the Resettlement Program. Just before I left, I learned that she and her family, unlike the majority of subjects I had interviewed, had been accepted for resettlement in the United States.

AMERASIANS
IN THE UNITED STATES

5 / Adapting to
Life in the United States

COMPARED TO OTHER VIETNAMESE IN THE UNITED STATES, Amerasians report more traumatic childhoods and less education in Vietnam.[1] They also report more present use of alcohol and continue to suffer more symptoms of trauma and depression than other Vietnamese. Despite these disadvantages, however, many Amerasians appear to be adapting well to life in the United States. Not surprisingly, Amerasians experiencing the most difficulty adjusting are those who speak English poorly, have little education, and are unemployed.[2] Compared to other Amerasians we will encounter in subsequent chapters, the two described here, a husband and wife, have adapted to American life remarkably successfully.

Natalie is a twenty-six-year-old white Amerasian woman who lives with her Amerasian husband and Vietnamese adoptive mother in a suburban apartment complex in a large American city. She flew from Vietnam to Thailand, spent one week there, and then trav-

1. Robert S. McKelvey and John A. Webb, "A Comparative Study of Amerasians, Their Siblings, and Unrelated Like-Aged Vietnamese," *American Journal of Psychiatry* 153 (1996): 561–63.

2. Emeka Nwadiora and Harriette McAdoo, "Acculturative Stress among Amerasian Refugees: Gender and Racial Differences," *Adolescence* 31 (1996): 477–87.

eled directly to the United States. She and her adoptive mother have lived in the same apartment since their arrival nine years ago.

All Natalie could tell me about her birth mother was that she knew how to read and write and came from a city northwest of Saigon. As her adoptive mother provided the following details about Natalie's birth, she sat next to her, listening intently.

Natalie was born in Saigon and given up at birth to her adoptive mother, a nurse who owned and operated an obstetrical clinic there. Her birth mother was already married to a Vietnamese Special Forces soldier and had two children by him. To earn extra money for the family, she went to work, against her husband's wishes, at a U.S. Army PX in Saigon. He was frequently away on maneuvers and apparently worried about what might happen to his wife if she were to work with American soldiers. He warned her that if she were to have an American's baby he would kill the entire family. At the PX, Natalie's birth mother met her father, a sergeant in the U.S. Army. When she became pregnant, she was unsure who the child's father was and felt understandably anxious. Since her husband was out of town at the time, she was able to make all the arrangements for the delivery herself. She came to Natalie's adoptive mother's obstetrical clinic and said to her, "if the baby is Vietnamese, I'll take it home with me; if it's Amerasian, I'll have to give it up." When the child, Natalie, proved to be Amerasian, she left her with Natalie's adoptive mother, went home, and told her husband that the delivery had been very difficult and the baby had died shortly after birth.

As Natalie listened to her adoptive mother tell the story, she began to cry. "It's so sad," she said, "especially about my mother's husband threatening to kill the family if the baby were an Amerasian."

From the time of her birth in 1971 until the fall of Saigon in 1975, Natalie enjoyed a very high standard of living. As owner and operator of an obstetrical clinic, her adoptive mother had five employees, including a doctor and a pharmacist, earned a lot of money, and even had a car, a Peugeot 203. However, after 1975 their lives changed greatly. According to her adoptive mother, "the Communists took over the clinic and made me an employee rather than the owner. Before, I'd been independent. Now I had to ask permission to do everything."

In 1977, when Natalie was six years old, her adoptive mother had to leave Saigon and return to her home town to care for her sister, who was paralyzed and very ill. She came from a very rich family there who, before 1975, had owned four hundred acres of paddy land. However, when the Communists came to power they took all their land, giving back one-tenth of an acre to each family member so they could raise some of their own food. Although the family's standard of living fell dramatically, they still had what Natalie's adoptive mother described as "a decent life with enough to eat," as they had some savings and were also able to sell coconuts from what remained of their land.

It was in her adoptive mother's home town, popularly known as "the cradle of Communists," that Natalie first learned she was different from other Vietnamese. When she started school, the children of Communists would beat her up and tell her to go to the United States because she was American. "As a child, my hair was very yellow, and the children called me *My-lai* (American half-breed). I wanted to dye my hair black, but my mother wouldn't let me." When she went to market older children chanted insulting phrases about Amerasians, saying, "Amerasians eat potatoes and beg—they eat in hiding because they're afraid of ghosts—Amerasians have twelve ass holes" (in Vietnamese, these insults rhyme and are selected more for that quality than for their logic or literary style). The taunting "made me angry at them, but all I could do was cry." At school, Natalie felt that her teachers discriminated against her openly. "I remember the teacher who was in charge of extracurricular activities. He didn't like me because I was Amerasian and made me do a lot of extra work, like cutting the grass and weeding, that other kids didn't have to do. He didn't say anything, but I could tell by his attitude that he didn't like me." In class, "teachers would ignore me, calling only on the Vietnamese kids." The teasing and discrimination made Natalie so unhappy that she wanted to quit school, but her adoptive mother would not let her.

Despite her problems at school, Natalie worked hard and was an excellent student. She was recognized and honored for her efforts by having her classmates select her deputy prefect from the first through the ninth grades. In this position she was responsible for organizing class activities such as drama, singing, and dancing. She also had a lot of friends, both at school and in her neighborhood. Her friends treated her kindly and did not tease. In retrospect, Natalie believes that it was mainly Communists and the children of Communists who treated her cruelly and practiced discrimination against her. "I don't like the Communists because they don't like me."

In postwar Vietnam discrimination was institutionalized. Even though she was an excellent student, Natalie was refused permission to take the high school entrance examination because she was Amerasian. As a result she had to leave school at age fifteen and stay at home helping her adoptive mother care for her elderly parents and sick sister. Seeing that Natalie had no prospects for a successful future in Vietnam, and learning of the Amerasian Resettlement Program, her adoptive mother applied on Natalie's behalf. Natalie remembers that "when she first talked about our going to the United States, I cried because I had no idea what it was like. But now I would never go back to Vietnam. In fact, I once had a dream that I went back and the Viet Cong caught me and forced me to stay. When I woke up I was so frightened that I resolved I would never return."

Even though she had studied English for a couple of years in Vietnam, after her arrival in the United States Natalie found things very difficult. "I'd go out and wouldn't understand anything people said to me. It was like I was deaf. Also, so many things were different. Bananas were bigger than those in Vietnam, and so were the watermelons. The markets were enormous. When I'd go there I'd get a strange feeling like someone from the countryside going to Saigon. I felt lost and confused. There are no such beautiful, well-organized markets in Vietnam. Some people from the YMCA took us to a shopping mall. It was beautiful! I remember stopping at McDonalds, buying a hamburger, and then not knowing how to eat it."

Natalie's primary aim in coming to the United States was to be able to continue her schooling and prepare for a meaningful career. She would like to be a nurse like her adoptive mother, "but not in obstetrics; I'd like to work in a general practitioner's office helping the doctor." She is currently enrolled in a local community college studying English, history, math, biology, and psychology. She eventually hopes to get a four-year nursing degree. While she likes going to school in the United States, she finds it very different from school in Vietnam. "In Vietnam students are more serious and industrious. You can't have boy friends and girl friends. Here there's no discipline. Everything is turned upside down. Teachers aren't shown respect; students don't care what the teacher says." She, herself, hasn't experienced any discrimination. "I'm just like everybody else; people think I'm Hispanic." However, she does believe many Vietnamese are discriminated against, especially by blacks. She has heard people teasing older Vietnamese when they think they cannot understand what is being said about them.

One year before I met her, Natalie married another Amerasian, a young man she met at a local store where they both worked as clerks. They had known each other four years before deciding to marry. Her husband had come to the United States alone—"some Vietnamese used him as a 'golden passport'"—and so they only had to ask permission of her adoptive mother. I asked what she would have done had her mother said no. "I know her. She'd never say no. But if she had, we'd have waited until she said yes."

Natalie has no interest in finding her biological parents. She knows nothing about her American father—not even his name—and has never attempted to locate him. She also never looked up her biological mother or two half siblings in Vietnam, although she knew where they lived. "It was just too far away."

As I completed my interview with Natalie and her adoptive mother, Natalie's Amerasian husband, Tom, arrived home from work. He is twenty-six years old, and to my eyes a strikingly handsome young man with such dominant Caucasian features one could easily mistake him for a white American. His English is excellent, far better than his wife's, and spoken with only a slight trace of accent. My interview with Tom was brief and does not present the same degree of detail provided by Natalie and her adoptive mother, but I have included it because of Tom's striking success at adapting to American life. His story illustrates both the special challenges faced by Amerasians who arrived in the United States unaccompanied and without family support, and the remarkable resilience shown by some of them in forging a new life alone and unassisted.

The only thing Tom knows about his American father is his first name, Jimmy. His mother had pictures of him, but when the Communists came to power she burned them, fearing reprisal. His father left Vietnam when his mother was pregnant and was never heard from again. For the first five years of his life, Tom lived with his mother and several of her friends in an apartment in Saigon. "They were all widows and loved one another like sisters. All of them treated me as if I were their son. I loved the oldest one most of all. She cooked special dishes for me and I'd go shopping with her, sitting on her lap in the cyclo. We had a very special relationship."

During this time, his mother, who never remarried, worked for the South Vietnamese government. When Saigon fell, she fled with Tom to her home village, where her two older Vietnamese children, a girl of twelve and a boy of seven, lived with her brother, who owned a farm. For the first few months in the village she kept Tom inside the house, hiding him for fear the Viet Cong would kill him because of his appearance. When the danger seemed to have passed, she left him with her brother and Tom's half siblings and returned to Ho Chi Minh City. Tom lived in the village for the next seven years. "My uncle took

74

good care of me, and having my brother and sister around helped soften the pain, but I still missed my mother very much."

In 1982, when Tom was twelve, his mother brought him back to Ho Chi Minh City to live again in the apartment with her and her friends. Tom's return had a special purpose—to prepare his escape from Vietnam. During the time his mother lived in the city without him she had encountered a family from her home village who lived near the farm where her brother was looking after Tom. They told her that they were desperate to leave Vietnam and had tried unsuccessfully to escape five times. Now they were planning to apply to immigrate legally to the United States under the Orderly Departure Program. "When my mother heard this, she became very emotional. She said, 'I have a son who is now twelve years old. I'd like for him to go to the U.S. He won't be able to find his father, but at least he'll have a better future.'" Tom's mother wanted to go, too, but had an eighty-year-old mother to care for and felt she had to remain in Vietnam. The family agreed to include Tom in their application, claiming he was their younger brother.

Tom and the family waited six years for their ODP interview. Tom recalls sitting in the interview session shaking with cold from the air conditioning, which he had never experienced before. Their application was approved, but it was another year before they were finally permitted to depart. They flew to Manila and were transported to the Philippine Refugee Processing Center. Asked how he felt upon his arrival there, Tom replied, "I cried a lot. Who wants to leave their home town? I cried for three nights. I missed my mom and familiar faces which had now disappeared. I wanted to go back to Vietnam. But then I made a lot of friends at the refugee camp and they helped me to feel better."

After eight months at the Philippine Refugee Processing Center, Tom and his new "family" were flown to the American city where he and Natalie now live. "When I first got here, everything seemed so strange. Part of me wanted to stay, part of me wanted to go back to Vietnam. Vietnamese I met here said that in this country people don't love or care for each other the way they do in Vietnam. When I heard that, I felt very sad."

Tom's early years in the United States were confusing and chaotic. For the first two years he and the family with whom he had migrated lived with another family in a very cramped apartment. Tom went to work for a local fish market, unloading fish from trucks. "I didn't like it. In Vietnam all I'd ever done was study and help my mother. I'd never worked, but I knew I had to do something to survive. The family I was living with didn't treat me kindly. They didn't support or help me. They had cash, food stamps, and Medicaid, but kept it all for themselves. They'd come here to get rich and all they ever thought about was money. I had to pay them for all my utilities and meals."

After Tom had spent three months at the fish market, a friend helped him get a job at an electronics company working as an assembler. Tom did this for six months, then met another Amerasian who was working on a shrimp boat. "He asked if I'd like to join him. I was twenty, but I wasn't very mature, thinking more like a twelve or thirteen year old. I just did what people told me and didn't think much about whether or not it was good for me. I quit my job without giving notice and went to work on the shrimp boat." Tom earned a lot of money catching shrimp, often as much as $200 per day, and was able to save most of it. After six months of this hard and isolated life, however, he had had enough and went back home to his "family." "When I returned, I had $6,000. I thought about going back to Vietnam. There was no one to give me advice. I finally decided to spend $3,400 for a car, then had to pay another $1,089 for insurance. I didn't know how to open a bank account, so I gave the rest of the money to the family. They just put it in their own account, and that was the last I saw of it. I was so naive and innocent. I knew nothing about life here, and had no idea how the system worked."

Tom was beginning to tire of life with the greedy family, who seemed only interested in exploiting him. "There were a lot of misunderstandings; they didn't know what I was really like. They thought I was the kind of Amerasian who just hangs around on the streets doing nothing." Finally he decided to move out and went to live with a stranger, a Vietnamese woman he had met who offered to let him live with her if he would help pay the rent. "She was a difficult woman. I thought at first that she loved me, but she tried to keep me inside all the time, restricting my contact with other people." He lived with her for a couple of years, then decided to move out, renting an apartment by himself.

Over the next few years Tom's life gradually began to assume greater direction and purpose. In addition to finding a stable job, first at a grocery supply company, then at the store where he and Natalie met, he resumed his education, enrolling in evening courses to learn English and computer skills. After a few years his English was good enough to enable him to enter community college and work toward a degree. The structure of school, a stable job, and especially his relationship with Natalie, seemed to steady him and give him purpose. By the time I met him he had become a supervisor at the store and was about to graduate from college. As I interviewed him, sitting proudly in a shirt and tie next to his wife at the dinner table of their comfortable apartment, Tom seemed to represent the quintessential American success story. He had arrived with nothing and received little or no support from the people around him. He had floundered for several years in a world he could not comprehend, moving from job to job, place to place, and relationship to relationship. Then, finally, he had found his feet, established himself in a career, secured an education, and created a family to love and support. How did he do it?

It is easy to understand how Amerasians, raised in poverty and deprived of love, support, and education, ended up among "the dust of life." But how is one to understand the success of an Amerasian like Tom? Clearly he possesses certain advantages. He is handsome, looks far more "American" than most other Vietnamese, has a gift for languages, and is a very able student. Yet he has also had his share of adversity: living apart from his mother, experiencing discrimination in postwar Vietnam, and being exploited by other Vietnamese after his arrival in the United States. Ultimately it is not possible to know the secret of his success. However, I discovered one quality in Tom that was not present in many Amerasians I interviewed, a sense of having been deeply loved as a child by his mother and those around him. This innate conviction that one is loved and lovable contributes powerfully to one's sense of self-worth. The Amerasians I interviewed who seemed to me least damaged psychologically by the poverty, prejudice, and discrimination that surrounded them during their early years in Vietnam were those who, like Tom, believed that they had been deeply loved by their mothers and other important adults in their lives. Perhaps it was the protective quality of his mother's love that enabled Tom to utilize his gifts and survive the many obstacles confronting him.

6 / Expectations
and Later Adjustment

IMMIGRANTS' EXPECTATIONS FOR LIFE IN A NEW COUNTRY CAN strongly influence their success at adapting and acculturating there. Generally, expectations based on a realistic appraisal of one's abilities and buttressed by plans to work hard are more likely to be achieved than grandiose and fanciful expectations. Simply assuming that one will become rich, without acquiring the skills and investing the effort to earn one's fortune, usually leads to disappointment and despair. Amerasians in Vietnam who had high hopes for their future lives in the United States were generally less depressed than those with low expectations.[1] However, when these same Amerasians were subsequently reassessed in the United States, those who had expected to receive high levels of support from the Vietnamese community in the United States were much more depressed than those who had expected little or no such support.[2] In addition to illustrating the complex relationship between expectations and mental health, these results imply that,

1. Robert S. McKelvey, Alice R. Mao, and John A. Webb, "Premigratory Expectations and Mental Health Symptoms in a Group of Vietnamese Amerasian Youth," *Journal of the American Academy of Child and Adolescent Psychiatry* 32 (1993): 414–18.
2. Robert S. McKelvey and John A. Webb, "Premigratory Expectations and Post-Migratory Mental Health," *Journal of the American Academy of Child and Adolescent Psychiatry* 35 (1996): 240–45.

in the United States as in Vietnam, Amerasians continued to receive little support from non-Amerasian Vietnamese.

The following stories suggest that modest, realistic expectations are more likely to be met, and lead to greater satisfaction with one's life, than expectations based on wishful thinking.

Tron is a thirty-four-year-old white Amerasian woman from central Vietnam. She knows nothing about her father other than that he was an American soldier. Prior to her relationship with Tron's father her mother had been married to a Vietnamese by whom she had three children, two girls and a boy. Tron does not know what happened to her mother's first husband. Shortly after Tron's birth, her mother married again, this time to an ethnic Chinese Vietnamese by whom she had four children, three boys and a girl.

Despite her mixed racial parentage and the presence of his own biological children, Tron's stepfather treated her well. "He loved me more than his own children, and still writes to me. Every time he writes he says that whenever he thinks of me he cries. He wants me to save my money so that I can come back and see him in Vietnam."

Tron has few memories of her early life. She remembers attending school, where she was well treated by both students and teachers. "It was the people on the street who called me names because I was Amerasian, not the kids at school." Tron did not enjoy school, describing herself as "lazy." Her parents enrolled her late, she was kept back several times, and by the age of fourteen, when her family moved to Ho Chi Minh City, she had only completed the third grade.

Tron does not know why they moved to the city, but suspects it may have been related to the many political and economic changes in Vietnam brought about by the Communist takeover in 1975. She completed three more years of school there, then quit for good, partly to help out at home, partly to escape the embarrassment of being a seventeen-year-old sixth grader. For the next three years Tron stayed at home, cooking and caring for the house and her younger half siblings. At age twenty she began to work for hire, helping to harvest the rice crop. She did not like the work, which was hot and tiring, but her family needed the money.

Tron continued as an agricultural laborer for the next three years, then at twenty-three married an ethnic Chinese Vietnamese from Cho Lon ("big market"), the commercial center of Ho Chi Minh City and, before the end of the war and the mass migration of thousands of "boat people," home to over a million ethnic Chinese. She was introduced to her husband by a friend. Tron had wanted to get married, and liked him because "he didn't drink alcohol or beer and only smoked a little." Despite the differences in their ethnic backgrounds, no objections were raised by either family. Tron's stepfather was himself ethnic Chinese, and her mother, who came originally from the north of Vietnam, spoke a little Chinese learned as a child. In addition, the elder brother of her new husband had recently married a young Vietnamese woman, and his family seemed to tolerate ethnic differences easily. The young couple moved into their own home, given to them by her husband's father. Her husband worked for a company in Cho Lon that recycled plastic sandals and earned enough money to provide them with a "sufficient" standard of living, a distinct improvement over the near poverty of her early years. Tron stayed at home to care for the house and raise their four children born over the next six years.

Tron first heard of the Amerasian Resettlement Program from neighbors in 1991. She went directly to the Foreign Affairs Bureau and applied, was quickly granted an interview, and in 1992 left with her husband and children for the Philippines. Life at the Philippine Refugee Processing Center was good. "All we had to do was study. They gave us food and clothing. Some of the black Amerasians used to get into fights after they'd been drinking, but I stayed out of it."

The family arrived in the United States in 1993, seven days after Tet, the Vietnamese celebration of the lunar new year. They lived initially in an apartment complex in the far southwestern suburbs of the city, moving after two years to their present apartment to be closer to public transportation. Her husband was able to find a job within two months of his arrival working as a butcher at a Chinese fish market. Tron did not work initially, but after a couple of years opened a licensed child care business in her home.

Tron had expected to find a better life in the United States and was not disappointed. Asked to describe how she feels about living in the United States, Tron used the expression *suong thay ba*. Literally, it means "as happy as if I were seeing my ancestors" and implies that one feels very happy. She went on to explain, "in Vietnam we were always hungry; here we have enough to eat." Her greatest concern prior to arrival was unemployment, but now that both she and her husband have jobs they are very content. "Life here is better when you have a job. When you do, you have nothing to worry about." She has experienced no discrimination and has found other Vietnamese, and especially Amerasians, to be very helpful, explaining how to enrol her children in school and how to ride the public transportation system.

The only recent sadness in Tron's life came with the death of her mother in Vietnam four months prior to our interview. She was informed by relatives shortly after her mother's death, but could not afford to return for the funeral. "I cried when I heard of her death, and I still cry when I think of her. She was sixty-five when she died, and spent her life taking care of eight children. She'd only had a couple of years of education, but could read, although she wrote very poorly. She's buried in a Buddhist temple near Ho Chi Minh City."

Tron is, in many ways, typical of those Amerasians I met who appeared to have adapted successfully to American life. Her life in Vietnam was difficult, but not so traumatic as to have damaged her forever. She was used to hard work, and came to the United States with the expectation that, if she got a job and applied herself, she would be happy. Compared to most Americans, she has a very restricted and modest life-style. She lives with her family in a two-bedroom apartment in a suburban housing complex far from the central city. Most of her neighbors are other Vietnamese immigrants, and she seldom leaves home other than to shop. Her apartment is decorated with inexpensive objects; colorful red calendars from Chinese markets and jewelers, Vietnamese lacquerware wall hangings and vases, plastic flowers, and several school photos of her children. It is comfortably furnished and has a VCR, stereo, and an enormous TV. She and her husband both work at low-income jobs with little prospect for advancement. They have no car and must rely on public transportation. Their children attend public schools. And yet, compared to life in Vietnam, her life in America is a vast improvement. The apartment has heat and air conditioning, the family has more than enough to eat, and they want for nothing important to them. While the average American might find this life not to his or her liking, for the average Vietnamese Amerasian it is far better than anything they had ever known or expected in Vietnam. Modest expectations appear to make for contentment.

T am is a thirty-two-year-old white Amerasian woman who has been in the United States for four years. Her mother was a Saigon native with a high school education who met Tam's American father when she was twenty-two. Tam does not know how they met. Her father, about whom she knows nothing, returned to the United States during her mother's pregnancy. After he left, Tam's pregnant mother met a Vietnamese man, fell in love, and quickly married. "My stepfather knew I wasn't his child, but he still loved me like my own father. When I was sick, it was he who cared for me, not my mother."

Tam was born in a small town near a coastal city. Her stepfather was a cook in the South Vietnamese army, and the family enjoyed an easy and comfortable life there for the first eleven years of Tam's life. Her parents never told her she was Amerasian, and when children at school called her *My-lai* (American half-breed) she said they were lying and fought back. When she asked her parents if she was Amerasian, they denied it, saying they were her birth parents. Only many years later, when she was twenty-six and being encouraged by her mother to apply for the Amerasian Resettlement Program, did Tam finally learn the truth about her birth.

Tam completed only two years of school. She was not much of a student and the other students' teasing got to her. "They teased me for being Amerasian and for being bigger than everyone else in the class. I'd get into fights every day. When I told the teacher about the teasing, he hit me for complaining. I got to the point where I hated school and always played hooky. Finally, I just quit and stayed home to help out with my two younger brothers."

When Tam was eleven her stepfather retired from the military and the family moved to Saigon. Life in the city was very difficult because her stepfather had a second family there and moved Tam's mother, who was the "little wife," into an apartment next door to the "big wife." Although he assured them things would be fine, they were not, and the two women quarreled constantly. The family had been in Saigon for only a few months when the city fell to the Communists. Shortly after the takeover the new government announced a campaign to "re-educate" former members of the South Vietnamese army. Not wanting to be sent to a re-education camp, and exhausted by the continuous tension between his two wives, Tam's stepfather decided to move the family to the countryside northeast of Saigon, where his father owned some land.

For the first few years their life in the country was very difficult. They worked as farmers on her grandfather's land, but severe flooding caused them to lose their crop twice. A fourth child was born, and to try to improve their lot her mother and stepfather began to supplement their income by smuggling logs. They got the logs near the coast, transported them by boat back to the town near their farm, and sold them to people interested in building houses. This illegal income made a big difference in their standard of living, and from then on the family's life was reasonably comfortable.

At the age of nineteen Tam was married to a neighbor, a young Vietnamese man whose parents were dead. Her parents arranged the marriage with his elderly aunt, and, although Tam was not enthusiastic about the young man, she decided she had better marry before it was too late. "In the country, if you don't get married by nineteen or twenty, people start to wonder if there's something wrong with you." Tam went to live with her new husband in his aunt's home, but quickly found she could not bear the old woman. "She was awful to me. I couldn't stand living with her, so after a year I left and went home, even though we already had a child. My husband came with me, but after three or four months he decided to go back to his aunt. At first my parents scolded me and told me I had to go back. But I kept refusing, and after a while they just accepted the fact that I'd be staying at home."

When Tam was twenty-six her mother and stepfather learned of the Amerasian Resettlement Program, told Tam of her American roots, and encouraged her to apply. Given the embarrassment caused by leaving her husband, Tam was eager to comply. She, along with her mother, daughter, stepfather, and two sisters, was accepted, and they departed from Vietnam in 1991. They stayed in the Philippines for nine months and arrived in the United States in June 1992, settling in the housing complex where I met her. Shortly after her arrival, Tam was introduced by a neighbor to a Vietnamese man about her age. A marriage was arranged, and five months later Tam was married for a second time. Smiling, Tam remarked, "I was glad to get married; it was a way to get revenge on my first husband."

Tam likes her life in the United States much better than her life in Vietnam. "I work for a Vietnamese dry cleaner. I'm hard working and serious, and my employer likes my work." Aside from going to work, Tam seldom leaves the apartment complex. "I go to work, come home, care for the kids, cook dinner, and go to bed." She likes the apartment complex where she lives, which has so many Vietnamese that it functions much like a Vietnamese village, even electing its own village chief. "Here in the apartment complex, people respect me. I've got some money, and if they ask me for something, I'm able to lend it to them." Her expectations for the future are modest. "My English is poor, so I'll never be a boss. I'd just like to continue working and earn enough money so I can save a bit and afford to help my family and friends in Vietnam."

I was interested to learn if Tam, who grew up thinking she was Vietnamese, thinks of herself as Vietnamese, American, or Amerasian. "I don't care about things like that. I'm a human being. All I want is to be a good person and live a good life."

Both Tron and Tam had modest and realistic expectations based on the assumption that, with hard work, they could get what they needed. The following story describes an Amerasian whose expectations have not been met and who, as a result, has ended up feeling unhappy and discouraged with her life in the United States.

Lien does not know her exact age because she was kidnapped from her birth mother as an infant. She thinks she is about twenty-nine. Her foster mother knew her birth mother, who had intended to give Lien up to her foster mother after birth. However, when she saw how pretty Lien was, with lovely curly hair, she decided to keep her, and would have done so if a kidnapper had not intervened. By a strange coincidence, the kidnapper sold Lien to her foster mother! Knowing she had been kidnapped, her foster mother searched for her birth mother to return the baby, but could not find her. As Lien related this unlikely story, she began to cry. "I'd like to be with my mother. I see other people with their mothers and I'd like to have one, too."

Lien knows nothing about either her birth mother or father. Judging from her strongly Caucasian features and fair skin, I would guess that her father was white. Her foster mother was unmarried when she purchased Lien, and the two of them lived with her foster mother's family, which consisted of her parents, brothers, and sister. Initially her foster mother wanted two Amerasian children, a girl and a boy, but Lien was so sickly that she decided to have only one. Lien does not know why her foster mother wanted Amerasian children, but thinks it was because of their light skin and curly hair, considered beautiful by the Vietnamese. Her foster mother owned a bar close to an American base in the Mekong Delta. U.S. soldiers often came to the bar, and one, noticing how pretty Lien was, offered to adopt her. When her foster mother refused to give her up, he offered to bring the entire family to the United States. Her foster mother refused this offer as well because she knew nothing of America and was afraid of what life there would be like.

When Lien was five years old her foster mother married a captain in the South Vietnamese army. He belonged to a medical unit and may have been either a doctor or a nurse. After her marriage, Lien's foster mother decided to leave Lien with her parents and move to her new husband's home, which was located in a town twenty miles away across the Mekong River. "I wanted to go with her, but she said I couldn't come. I felt very sad. On her wedding day, I accompanied her to her husband's home, and when it was time to leave I refused to go. I begged her not to leave me, but eventually I was forced to go home."

Unfortunately, her foster mother's marriage did not work out well. Lien visited her every two or three months and remembers how the new husband tied her foster mother up and beat her. He also kept a concubine, "treating her more like his wife and my foster mother more like his concubine." Her foster mother often came home to visit her parents and Lien, tearfully telling them how cruel her husband was. (Lien recently learned that she had finally divorced him a couple of years ago).

After her foster mother left home, Lien gradually began to adjust to life without her. She was closest to her foster grandfather, as her foster grandmother was kept very busy with her business. She sold *mam,* the small, anchovylike fish, very popular in Vietnam, which is the main ingredient of the national fish sauce, *nuoc mam.* In the years before the end of the war, Lien's foster grandparents lived quite comfortably and were able to buy whatever they needed from the nearby U.S. base.

Lien recalls, for example, how as a young child she did not care for rice. Despairing of what to feed her, her foster grandparents finally arranged to give her milk and orange juice as an alternative. After the war's end, however, their standard of living fell dramatically. The family had to survive on the rice they could raise on two acres of paddy land along with vegetables from their garden. As Lien recalls, "there was enough to eat, but it wasn't like before when we had everything we wanted."

Lien completed only three years of school, leaving partly because she did not like it and partly because she was bigger than the other kids, which made her feel uncomfortable. Although she was teased for being Amerasian, it did not bother her, because she experienced the teasing as more good natured than cruel. For a time after she left school, her grandfather hired a tutor so she could continue her studies, but eventually they could no longer afford it and she spent her time helping with the house, garden, and rice crop.

As she grew older and entered her teens, Lien sensed her grandfather's eagerness for her to marry. "He was afraid that if I didn't marry soon, I'd fall prey to the tricks of bad boys and he'd end up with a single mother under his roof." She quoted a proverb suggesting that having a young, unmarried woman in one's house "is like having a large *mam* bowl hanging over the head of your bed" (the bowl might fall on your head while you sleep). He was therefore relieved when, at the age of nineteen, she received a marriage proposal from a young Vietnamese man she had met while visiting a cousin. She was soon married and went to live with her new husband's family.

Lien's husband was a schoolteacher, and the family's standard of living was not as high as that of her foster grandparents. "They didn't have enough money or rice, and I had to help my mother-in-law make and sell rice paper for egg rolls." Her new husband's family treated her kindly, however, and she lived with them happily, giving birth to her first child, a girl, before leaving Vietnam.

In 1989, when she was twenty-one, Lien and her husband applied for the Amerasian Resettlement Program because they "wanted to have a better life." She said she hoped that in the United States "we'd get good jobs, make lots of money, and be able to help our family in Vietnam." They were accepted to the program in 1990, spent six months at the Philippine Refugee Processing Center, where her second child, a boy, was born, and arrived in the United States in December 1990.

Lien and her family have always lived in the same apartment. Their friends are predominantly ethnic Chinese Vietnamese whom they met after arriving in the United States. She also has Amerasian and other Vietnamese friends, but knows very few Americans because she spends most of her time in the apartment complex caring for her four children, two of whom were born after her arrival. She is further limited by her poor English and because she does not know her way around the city. Her husband is the family's sole breadwinner. This is a cause for great concern, because it limits their income and makes them vulnerable if he were to get sick or lose his job. Even with him working, their resources are stretched caring for four children, and they are constantly short of money. She has just begun to receive food stamps, after a lengthy delay caused by her ignorance of how to apply, and their children are all covered by Medicaid. She and her husband, however, are not covered and have no other form of health insurance. Thus money and illness are constant and recurring concerns. Lien also worries that her unfamiliarity with "the system" will cause her to neglect to do something important and that as a consequence she and her children will lose their benefits. She wishes there were someone to help her find her way through the bureaucratic maze.

Although Lien continues to hope that she and her husband will earn a lot of money in the United States, she is beginning to realize that their dreams may not come true. In addition to all the difficulties of supporting their nuclear family, Lien's foster mother back in Vietnam was recently diagnosed with hepatitis, and her mother-in-law is old and ill. Lien and her husband send whatever money they can back to Vietnam, both to support their aging mothers and to pay for her brothers and sister to learn English so that one day they, too, can come to live in the United States.

All of these demands on their very limited income leave Lien depressed and discouraged. Stuck in a low-paying job, Lien's husband has little chance for advancement, and until the children are old enough so that she, too, can work, their future prospects appear quite constricted. Compared to her dreams of what life in the United States would be like, her present reality leaves much to be desired.

7 / Disabled Amerasians

THE IMPLICATIONS OF DISABILITY IN VIETNAM, WHETHER physical, mental, or emotional, are different and more difficult than they are in the developed Western world. In traditional Vietnamese society, disability brings shame both to the disabled person and to his or her family. Severe mental illness, for example, is viewed as a punishment for bad deeds in this or a past life and signifies the gods' disfavor.[1] As a result, families with a disabled member often hide the person away to avoid the shame of the disability, rather than explore rehabilitation. Although this attitude is slowly changing, and programs to assist disabled people are gradually being developed in Vietnam's larger cities, Amerasians grew up at a time when disability often meant a lifetime of shame, neglect, and, at times, abandonment. Added to the stigma of being Amerasian in postwar Vietnam, the burden of disability could prove overwhelming for a young person's development.

Although people with disabilities have more opportunities for rehabilitation in the United States than in Vietnam, immigrants with disabilities still face enormous challenges. For example, the entry level jobs available to unskilled immigrants often involve heavy lifting, which may prove impossible for those with physical disabilities. Simi-

---

1. Tran Minh Tung, *Indochinese Patients* (Washington, D.C.: Action for South East Asians, 1980).

larly, those with little English are unable to take advantage of opportunities to work in fields requiring basic communications skills. The
following stories illustrate the attempts of three Amerasians with disabilities to find meaningful work in the United States.

D am is a thirty-two-year-old black Amerasian born in Saigon. He
was abandoned at birth and knows nothing of his biological
parents. The woman who became his foster mother had recently lost
two children to disease and superstitiously believed that if she took him
in her five other children would be healthy. After Dam went to live
with her, however, his foster mother's sisters raised objections because
he was black, and so she gave him to her own mother, who was wid-
owed and lived with an elderly aunt. Dam lived with his foster grandmother until he was four or five, when he was returned to his foster
mother, who wanted him to help care for her children.

When the war ended in 1975, Dam was ten years old. The new
Communist government had instituted a policy of encouraging resi-
dents of Ho Chi Minh City to move to the country to alleviate over-
crowding in Vietnam's largest city. His foster mother agreed to return
to her home village, about sixty miles away, which she had left during
the war because of heavy fighting in the region. Dam remained in the
city with one of his older foster sisters so that he could continue his
schooling. Two years later, the foster sister married and Dam rejoined
his foster mother in the country.

Dam lived in his foster mother's home village from the age of
twelve until he left for the United States in 1993 at the age of twenty-
eight. He had completed third grade in Ho Chi Minh City, but once
he got to the village decided not to continue his schooling. Initially he
explained this decision as a practical one—he had to earn a living—but
he later revealed that it had been prompted by the cruel teasing he
received from many villagers. In Ho Chi Minh City, there were other
Amerasians and, although people on the street did begin to call him
names after the Communist takeover, the taunting was much less se-

vere than it was in the countryside, where he was the only black person around. Everywhere he went, villagers called him *My den* (black American) and *My lai* (American half-breed), making him feel unhappy and inferior. At first he bore the pain stoically, but as he grew older he began to shout back and argue with his tormentors, saying, "I don't tease you, why do you tease me? If you don't stop, I'll tell your parents."

Life in the country was very hard. He helped his foster family work their land, hiring himself out between harvests to make extra money. "I don't think I had a moment of happiness there. I worked hard, didn't have enough to eat, and couldn't save anything for the future. It rained a lot, and I had to work outside in the sun and rain without any time to rest. My life was worse than some and better than others. There were a lot of people like me who had to work very hard just to earn enough to stay alive."

Dam says he never had any close friends in Vietnam. "I'd get along with people for a few days, then there would be quarrels about money lent and not returned. A friend is someone who's there in times of need. The only person who was really friendly to me was twenty years older than myself. He taught me a lot; there was nothing I could learn from younger people."

At the age of twenty-one, Dam was apprenticed to a carpenter a few miles from his home. There he met a neighbor girl and, after an acquaintance of six or seven months, decided to marry. "I asked my mother to talk to her mother. She was happy for us to marry, as she wanted her daughter to be able to go to the United States." The young couple had two children in Vietnam and a third born after their arrival in the United States.

Dam and his family left Vietnam in August 1993 and, after six months at the Philippine Refugee Processing Center, arrived in the United States in February 1994. "I wanted to leave Vietnam because life there was very hard. I knew I'd have to work here, but I thought it would be easier to make a living." Initially, however, Dam experienced considerable difficulty finding work. He has a hearing impairment and found that, once potential employers learned of his disability, they did not want to hire him. "Because of my hearing problem, people think I can't work well, but they're wrong. For someone like me to get work, I have to really excel, so I'm better than the average worker." Three or four months after his arrival, two Mormons came to his door. "They asked if I needed help. I told them, 'if you want to help, help me find a job.' " They did, and in gratitude he became a Mormon.

His first job was installing tiles, and he earned $5 an hour. "I really worked hard, applied myself, and now make $12 an hour." He would like to open his own business but, because of his hearing, cannot talk on the phone. "In Vietnam doctors said the problem wasn't in my ear, but in my nervous system. I'd hoped I might be able to get it fixed in the U.S., but the doctors here don't know what the problem is. They told me they can't fix it, and recommended I buy a hearing aid, but it doesn't work." Dam showed me the hearing aid, which sits in its case along with other valuable artifacts on the family altar.

Aside from difficulty finding work because of his hearing, Dam has not experienced discrimination in the United States. "Here, I'm not the only black man." Although he sees himself as black, he does not identify strongly with any racial or ethnic group. "I don't think about that. All I think about is working, getting money, raising and educating my children, and making a better future for them. The most important thing in my life is my responsibility as a parent."

Asked if he misses Vietnam, Dam replied, "no, I don't miss anything about it. I do hope that some day I can save enough money to return and see my foster mother. After she dies, there's nothing else to draw me back."

Despite the opportunity to work and educate his children, Dam has some reservations about life in the United States. "Here, people only want to get money. Feelings, friendship, and love aren't important to them, so there's a lot of competition and conflict. Each person wants to go up and, to do so, feels he has to push others down." Asked how this affects him, Dam told a story. "Once I was hired to build a basketball court. I worked with a white American to put down the floor. It took us a day to do it. The person who was overseeing the job told us to nail the boards down. When we did, he told the boss we didn't know what we were doing; we should have glued them down. I think he did it just to get the work for himself. I don't like that kind of competition, but I have to cope with it. My fee is $12 an hour, but if somebody underbids me, I'll lower my fee. The bottom line is, I've got to have work. Once I do, there's no problem."

It was winter when I interviewed Dam, and the day was gray, cold, and wet. "I get worried at this time of year, because it's so cold there's no work laying tiles. As a result, I'm underemployed and can't make enough money to support my family." I asked if he discusses his concerns with anyone. "No, I've learned to keep my worries to myself. When I first came here and was looking for work, I'd tell people about my hearing problem. They'd tell potential employers, who wouldn't hire me because of my disability. Now I've learned to keep things to myself."

Like the weather, Dam's apartment was bleak and cold. There were many stains in the rug, the furniture was old and second hand, and the room's only decorations were a few plastic flowers and a red Chinese calendar. Seated in these grim and unpretentious surroundings on the distant outskirts of an American city, Dam impressed me as a proud and determined man. He was particularly pleased that, in just three years, his income had risen from $5 to $12 an hour. As his children walked in and out of the room, he interacted with them gently and lovingly. Asking little of life, he seemed grateful for whatever good fate and hard work might bring him.

When I met Tuong she was twenty-eight, very pregnant, and expecting the birth of her fourth child within the next few days. Her vocabulary was quite limited, and she seemed to have a lot of trouble remembering the details of her past life. She ascribed her memory problems to the fact that she is illiterate, but the interpreter and I wondered if she might also suffer from an intellectual handicap.

Tuong was born in Ho Chi Minh City. She knows nothing of her American father, who left Vietnam during her mother's pregnancy. Her mother has told her that he wanted them to come with him to the United States, but she did not want to leave her father. Tuong was the second child born of her mother's relationship with the American. The older child is a boy, handicapped with "a condition that left one arm withered and a hunch on his left hip." Her mother cleaned homes and, because of Tuong's brother's handicap, was the family's sole source of support, aside from some savings she had accumulated during her time with Tuong's father. The family's poverty compelled Tuong to begin working at age five, and she never attended school. "I wanted to go to school like everybody else, but my mother said if I did we wouldn't have enough money to survive." Tuong's job was to sell sweet potatoes and manioc to students.

Tuong, her mother, and her brother lived in Ho Chi Minh City with her maternal grandfather. He and her maternal grandmother had separated when Tuong's mother was very young. Her grandmother moved to Ho Chi Minh City with Tuong's mother while her grandfather remained in his home village. He visited his wife and daughter every few weeks, but the couple never got back together again. Tuong knows very little about her mother's early life other than that she could read and write Vietnamese and spoke a little English. When Tuong was eighteen her grandfather, who had come to live in Ho Chi Minh City with her mother, became ill and wanted to return to his home village. The family moved with him, but because he no longer owned a house there, they had to live with relatives. They supported themselves by hiring out as agricultural laborers, moving from relative to relative so as not to become too much of a burden. Tuong remembers this period as the most miserable of her life. They were even poorer than they had been in Ho Chi Minh

City, and there was never enough food or clothing. One year they earned so little that they could not afford to buy rice, the staple of the Vietnamese diet, and were reduced to eating manioc and vegetables they could glean from the fields. As Amerasians Tuong and her brother were often taunted as half-breeds. Their mother was insulted for having an affair with an American, and when she walked by people would chant a demeaning phrase, *tam bay tam ba* (wherever you go, you do the wrong thing). Finally, after several years of this downtrodden, destitute, and thoroughly desperate existence, her mother was able to persuade her brother, a policeman, to arrange for them to move back to Ho Chi Minh City.

Their return to the city brought a marked improvement in their standard of living. All three were now able to find employment. Her mother returned to cleaning houses, her brother worked for a manufacturer of cooking utensils, and Tuong became a street vendor of water and soft drinks. In her spare time, Tuong also cleaned plastic bags for recycling. She remembers this as the best period of her life in Vietnam, for at last they had enough food and clothing.

In Ho Chi Minh City Tuong met the young Vietnamese who was to become her husband. He was employed as a glass blower and, by Tuong's standards, was fairly well to do. They were introduced by her policeman uncle and courted for two years. "I loved him and he loved me. My mother accepted the marriage and said it was up to me." Despite the fact that she was Amerasian and poor, her boy friend's family loved her and raised no objections to their marriage. The wedding was a very small affair, because Tuong's family could not afford to contribute anything and all expenses had to be borne by the groom's family.

Asked why she had left Vietnam, Tuong responded, "there was a rumor going around that all Amerasians had to leave the country. My mother believed the rumor. She was afraid that if we didn't apply for resettlement, we'd be forced to leave like the boat people. That just seemed too risky, so we applied."

97

Tuong expected life in the United States to be better than life in Vietnam. "I imagined I'd be happy here. I thought I'd have enough to eat and could eat whatever I wanted. If I wanted to eat an apple, I could eat an apple. If I wanted to eat meat, I could eat meat." Generally, Tuong has not been disappointed, but there are problems. "Only my husband works, plus I get $300 a month in food stamps for the kids. My husband earns $700 a month, and that's just enough for what we need. The apartment costs $400 a month, then there's $50 for heat, $150 for air conditioning, plus the telephone. At the end of the month, there's nothing left. If he lost his job, it'd be a catastrophe. We'd have to move out of our apartment. What's not good about the United States is when you don't have enough money. You can't borrow from your neighbors like in Vietnam." To help support the family, her mother, who is now fifty-seven, has gone back to work cleaning houses. She lives-in at the house where she cleans, and returns to see Tuong and the family every few weeks.

Tuong has no desire to return to Vietnam. "One day when the children are grown up and have jobs, I hope they'll give me money to visit Vietnam one last time. I'd like to visit my husband's family and my relatives, and maybe see some of our neighbors."

Minh is a twenty-six-year-old Amerasian with no formal education, but who is able to read and write Vietnamese.[2] He came to the United States two years ago and has never been employed here.

His father worked in Vietnam for an American construction company. When his contract ended in 1968, he left behind Minh and his mother, who was four months pregnant. Between 1968 and 1975, the family's income came from three sources—money the father had left behind, money he continued to send from the United States, and the mother's job. Their standard of living did not decline precipitously, as

2. This is the only interview I did not conduct personally. It was done by a Vietnamese colleague, Thien-Kim Pham.

was the case for many Amerasians after the departure of their fathers, and they were able to lead a fairly comfortable life. Minh, however, contracted polio as a young child, and his mother spent a lot of their savings getting him treatment.

When the Communists came to power in 1975 life changed drastically for Minh and his family. Payments from his father ended abruptly as mail service between the United States and Vietnam became unreliable. To protect herself and the family, his mother destroyed all evidence connecting her with her American husband. However, since she had two obviously Amerasian children, she was forced to relocate to a New Economic Zone. The place to which they were sent was a remote piece of land in the jungle which had never been cultivated before. They were given nothing and had to survive on whatever they could carry with them. They arrived with three cartloads of personal possessions. After three years of poverty, hard work, and disease, they finally escaped back to his mother's home town. On their return all they owned could now be fitted into one small gym bag. Everything else had been sold off, piece by piece, in exchange for food and clothing.

Their homecoming was a disaster. The people in his mother's home town wanted nothing to do with her; she had two Amerasian children, no money, and no possessions. She was also malnourished, depressed, and too sick to work. As a result, Minh, at the age of eleven, had to work full time to support the family. For the next five years he [collected garbage and cleaned toilets]. Speaking of his life then, Minh began to cry. The work was humiliating, one of the worst of jobs in Vietnam and taken only by those too poor to have any other options. His boss treated him cruelly, calling him names and barely feeding him. The nature of his work, along with his handicap, also brought the jibes of other Vietnamese, who called him a "retarded Amerasian."

In 1983 his mother's uncle, a high Communist official, took pity on them and moved them to the city. He refused to provide them with any material support, however, so their standard of living did not improve. Everyone in the family worked, taking whatever jobs they could find. Their income was so low and irregular that they had to move frequently and several times ended up living on the streets. Minh struggled to survive, knowing his mother and sister depended on him, but at times he found his life unbearable and began to drink as an escape.

In 1985 Minh and his family returned to his mother's home town. There they heard Amerasians were being relocated to the United States. They were initially reluctant to apply, fearing it might endanger her uncle's career if members of his family were to flee the country, but in 1988 the uncle became ill and resigned from his post. Minh and his family took advantage of this opportunity and applied for the Amerasian Resettlement Program. It took four years to negotiate the corrupt and inefficient bureaucracy in Vietnam, and it was not until early 1994 that Minh and his family finally arrived in the United States.

They were sponsored by a resettlement agency and placed in an apartment complex with many other recent Vietnamese immigrants where they began to receive welfare checks and food stamps. Because of his disability, Minh also qualified for disability benefits, which helped supplement the family's income. Given the misery of his years in Vietnam, Minh's expectations for life in the United States were very modest. He did not expect to get rich or find his father. All he wanted was food, clothing, shelter, and the possibility of earning the respect he was denied in Vietnam.

These modest expectations were largely met, but now that Minh has been in the United States for a while, he has begun to look around and compare himself with other Vietnamese. Many, especially those who arrived in the late 1970s and early 1980s, have their own homes, good jobs, nice cars, and lovely clothes. Minh sees that his life does not measure up and knows that he still has a long way to go, but he does not know how to get there. He has a physical disability, no vocational skills, and he cannot speak English. He is taking an English course at the YMCA, but had no formal education in Vietnam and does not know how to study. His social contacts are entirely with other Vietnamese in the apartment complex, who, like himself, are relative newcomers to the United States and have few contacts outside their local community. Minh spends most of the day eating, watching TV or videos, and hanging out with other Vietnamese in the apartment complex. He often feels bored, but does not really know what to do with himself. All his basic needs are met, so there is not the daily struggle for survival that at least kept him going in Vietnam. Being poor, unemployed, Amerasian, and disabled, Minh feels that he still has not been able to earn the respect he desires. He would like to get out and explore the world around him, but does not have a car or enough English to feel confident outside the complex. Much of the time he feels trapped and useless. Still, he would not want to go back to Vietnam, except, perhaps, for a visit. And if he did return, it would only be to get revenge on all those who treated him and his family poorly.

In the future Minh hopes to get a car modified for his disability so that he can get out and experience the United States and earn a lot of money. The key to everything, he believes, is to learn English well so that he can get a good job. Alternatively, he dreams of winning the lottery, which would be a quicker and easier path to the fulfillment of his dreams.

Minh's disability and his lack of formal education, vocational training, and English language skills, have all made it difficult for him to take advantage of the opportunities available in the United States. He also continues to suffer emotionally from the years of hatred and persecution he experienced as an Amerasian in Vietnam, from his family's miserable existence in the New Economic Zone, from their struggle to survive in Vietnam's collapsing postwar economy, and from the stigma and shame of the terrible jobs he had to do in Ho Chi Minh City. At times he feels quite depressed and can see no way out. He often wonders if he will ever feel truly happy.

8 / Searching for Father

COMMON TO THE LIVES OF ALMOST ALL AMERASIANS WAS THE loss of their American father. While a few Americans took long-term responsibility for their children, most did not, leaving mother and child to fend for themselves. Growing up fatherless in a society like Vietnam's, where status, income, and opportunity derive from the father, Amerasians faced almost insurmountable difficulties. As adults, Amerasians express a variety of feelings toward their American fathers. Some are understandably bitter and angry, others wonder what he was like and enshrine him in respectful fantasies, and still others are indifferent. In Vietnam many express a wish to find him once they are in the United States, but few have enough information to make this more than a wish. A very few—perhaps 2 or 3 percent—actually locate their American fathers and reunite with them. Such reunions are often not successful. Their fathers have gotten on with their lives, marrying, having other children, and all but forgetting long-ago affairs and relationships. They are reluctant and concerned to be confronted by an adult child, whom most knew only as a baby, if at all.

The following stories illustrate different aspects of Amerasians' search for their fathers. In the first, an Amerasian still in Vietnam yearns for reunion, hoping that his American father will make right the many years during which he suffered poverty and discrimination. In the second, an Amerasian in the United States, reunited with her American father, must deal with the reality of their relationship and its inevitable disappointments.

D uring our interview, Tang appeared to me to be tense and angry, answering questions briefly and with little detail. He is a twenty-six-year-old Amerasian and has lived all his life in Ho Chi Minh City. He knows little about his biological mother and has no memories of her. She abandoned him when he was very young. He has been told that she worked for the Americans, met his American father, and became pregnant by him. During her pregnancy Tang's father left for the United States. Tang was raised by foster parents. Asked how he came to live with them, Tang responded, "I don't know. My foster mother probably felt pity for me." At the time she adopted him his foster mother was forty or fifty years old and already had a biological son who was older than Tang. Her husband, Tang's foster father, died when Tang was a child, and he does not remember him.

Tang's foster mother supported the family by selling broken bottles that she collected on the street. Their standard of living was very low. She could not afford to send him to school, and so Tang spent his childhood helping her collect bottles and assisting with household chores. "Our house was not very clean. We were the lowest class in society. We did have some furniture and I slept in a bed. I had a few clothes and we had just enough food to live."

When he was about eleven years old Tang began to realize that he looked different from other Vietnamese. His foster brother and other children teased him about his appearance. "They'd say, 'you're American, not Vietnamese.' They'd chant, '*My lai muoi hai lo dit*' (Amerasians have twelve assholes) and I'd feel very angry. But there wasn't much I could do because there were so many of them. It made me feel ashamed. I talked with my foster mother about the teasing, but she couldn't do anything about it. I asked her if I could leave the country with other Amerasians, but she wouldn't let me." Tang wonders if part of the reason his mother did not send him to school was because of the discrimination she thought he would experience at the hands of his teachers and other children.

Tang believes that his foster mother loved him very much. "She liked me more than her own son. I could tell she did because she'd give me candy and not give him any. When I told her he called me American she'd scold him."

Two years before I met Tang his foster mother died. After her death his foster brother kicked him out of the house and Tang had to live on the streets or in the houses of friends. He supported himself mixing cement for construction projects. The work was short term and did not pay well, but it was the only work he could get. One month before we met, Tang had come to the Amerasian Transit Center hoping to gain acceptance into the Resettlement Program. He had not yet officially applied for the Program and did not have permission to stay in the Center, but an Amerasian friend took him in and Center staff allowed him to remain. He kept in touch with his foster brother, but their contact was minimal. "We don't get along. We're like strangers. It has always been that way."

Tang has a girl friend, a full Vietnamese whose parents do not accept him. "They don't like me because I'm Amerasian and not a full Vietnamese. Her father is a Communist and he hates me because of my American blood." Tang has never met his girl friend's parents. "A friend told me that they don't like me and I shouldn't go to their house. If they continue not to like me I may have to break up with my girl friend. We just can't go on like this. When we see one another we're happy, but I can't promise to do anything for her yet because my life is not normal. She's twenty-nine, works for a tailor, and has a good standard of living." At this point the interpreter interrupted. "I spoke with his girl friend last week. She's a nice north Vietnamese girl. She told me, 'I really love this guy, but my family is so strict. At first I thought he had some education, but it turns out he can't read or write. I feel so sorry for him.' She loves him and he loves her, but what can you do? Her father died recently so maybe there's some hope."

Tang's dream is to go the United States and find his American father. "I'm hoping that a charitable organization will help me find him.
I want to tell him about my suffering. I want to tell him how I've been
treated here. I want to be close to him. Right now, the only person I'm
close to is my girl friend."

Tang hopes that reunion with his American father will put an end to
the poverty and discrimination of his life in Vietnam. However, Tang
is very far from the realization of his dream. He knows nothing of his
American father. He has no photo of him, does not know his name or
anything about his appearance, and does not even know the unit in
which his father served in Vietnam. At the time we met, Tang had not
even applied for the Amerasian Resettlement Program and it was coming rapidly to an end. When he asked me if I could help him find his
American father I could not think of anything to say. There seemed to
be no way for his dream of reunion to come true, but I did not want to
shatter that dream and take away his only hope for a happy future.

Q uyen lives in a public housing complex on the outskirts of a
large American city. Her neighbors are primarily blacks, Lati-
nos, and other Vietnamese immigrants who earn their living as laborers
or working at unskilled, entry-level jobs. My interpreter and I arrived
at the complex after dark and had to search for her apartment in a
warren of nearly identical buildings. We knocked at a dimly lit door
opened by a young girl, who invited us in and introduced us to
Quyen's mother, a diminutive woman in her mid- to late forties, casu-
ally dressed in slacks and blouse, whose raven-black hair was tinged
with gray. Friendly and engaging, she made us comfortable, offered us
drinks, and apologized for her daughter's late arrival. "She's on her way
back from school and the traffic is very heavy this evening." The interpreter explained to her my long-standing interest in Amerasians and
other Vietnamese, my work with Vietnamese refugees, and my desire
to write a book describing the Amerasian experience. Quyen's mother
asked if I myself had children. When I acknowledged that I did, she

said, "God will bless them for the interest you have shown in the problems of the Vietnamese."

While we waited for Quyen to arrive, her mother began to tell us about herself. "I suffered a lot of shame and dishonor before and after the war. People looked down on me for having a foreign husband." At that moment Quyen came in the door, and we rose to greet her. She was a slender young woman, about five feet tall, and wearing the student's uniform of blue jean slacks and jacket and a light-blue denim shirt. Her hair was long and dark brown, not black like her mother's, and she had more Caucasian features—lighter skin, rounder brown eyes, and a more highly bridged nose. The scars of acne were faintly visible on her attractive, open face. After a brief discussion of how to proceed, I decided to interview Quyen alone, as her English was very good, while her mother and the interpreter conversed at the other end of the room.

Quyen and I realized we had met several years before at a gathering for Vietnamese Amerasians. She told me she was now twenty-six years old and a nursing student at a local community college. "I've been there for three years and still have a couple more years to go. I changed my major from pre-med because I didn't like physics and lost some credits. That's why it's taking me so long." I explained the purpose of my visit, described the book I was writing, and asked if she would be willing to let me use her story as part of it. She agreed, and asked how we should begin. I asked if she could tell me about her parents' relationship.

"My mother worked in a canteen at an American base where my father was a helicopter pilot. He flew the helicopters with red crosses that rescue the wounded. He was married at the time, but my mother didn't know that. She was about three months pregnant with me when he was transferred to another American base. She never heard from him again." I asked how her mother's parents had reacted to her relationship with an American. "They were very mad and sad. My family is strict and traditional. You have to marry before you get pregnant, especially if the man is a foreigner. All their friends looked down on our family. In Vietnam people are very nosy. My mother was forced to leave home by her parents. They told her to give me away, but she said no. They said, 'give the baby away or leave the house.' She went to another city and worked as a housekeeper for a woman who was also married to an American. After a while my great-grandfather went looking for her. He lived with her parents because his oldest son was her father and had to care for him. He took her back home and convinced his son to let her stay. I was born at home. After I was born, they pressured her again to give me away, but she refused and took me to live with her at a friend's house. Every night she'd go back home and visit her parents. She went at night so that people wouldn't see her. After a few months, my grandparents relented and let us come home."

I asked Quyen how she had learned about her parent's relationship. "I found out quite late. I never asked. I remember one day I was giving my mother a hard time about something. I talked back to her. We never did things like that in my family. She cried and was angry and told me what had happened. I was sixteen then. She'd always told me my father was a nice, lovely man, but it wasn't nice to cheat on his wife and lie to my mother." I asked how the knowledge of the truth about her parent's relationship had affected her. "I loved my mother more. I felt I should pay her more respect because she had gone through so much trouble for me." How had it made her feel about her father? "I never felt hatred in my heart. I was so innocent at the time. My mother always said he was a great guy. She believed he'd come back and bring us here, but he never came. She waited for twelve years."

Asked to describe her life growing up in Vietnam, Quyen said, "I remember when I was three years old. It was the time when the North Vietnamese came. They forced all Amerasians and their families to leave their homes and go to the New Economic Zones. I remember my grandmother carrying me in a bamboo basket on a pole over her shoulder with her belongings balanced at the other end. My mother was walking behind us. We had to walk a long way to get to the NEZ; I think it was about forty kilometers. I kept praying for a car to come and pick us up, but the cars didn't go that far down the road. When we got to the place, there was no house for us. They just gave us a piece of land. My mother, grandparents, uncle, and auntie had to build a house. I lived there until I left Vietnam. I still miss the place a lot, compared to the big city. The schools weren't very good. I had to walk a couple kilometers to school, and when it rained hard, I had to swim part of the way! My friends in school called me names. They'd say, 'you're an Amerasian (*My lai*). Where's your father? He left you. He doesn't love you.''

I asked when she had first realized she was different. "When I went to school. They called me names, so I fought back. My mother used to try to make up for my being different by dressing me up very well. I was always the best dressed student in the school. Everyone thought we must be rich and that my father was supporting me because of my nice clothes. All the instructors loved me. I'm lucky because I was pretty bright compared to the other students there. I loved to sing and dance. I'd sing at the school festivals. I remember once a lot of Montagnards came to a festival. When I started to sing they were sitting far away, but after a while they came up close to listen to me.

I asked Quyen how being an Amerasian had affected her. "A lot. I didn't realize it at the time, but I do now. I missed having the love of a father. I also didn't get the opportunity to do things I wanted to do. I was very good in school. In ninth grade I was supposed to join the Communist youth group. It was an honor and very important if you wanted to get ahead. But there was one teacher from the North. She managed to delay my entry into the group for one year. She said that because my father was an American and I was an Amerasian my background wasn't very good. I told her, 'my father was American, but I'm Vietnamese. I've done nothing wrong.' The other instructors at the school were from the same part of Vietnam I am. They supported me, and I finally got in.''

I asked if she had encountered any other difficulties growing up. "My mother had a small grocery store in the village. I helped out by working in the store, planting and harvesting rice, and going to the mountains to get firewood. It was a hard life. In the first few years the Communists gave us rice, but there was mold and insects in it. Then my family started to plant rice, vegetables, sweet potatoes, and manioc. I ate a lot of sweet potatoes and manioc. The government demanded that we give them rice to pay for the land. So we had to mix sweet potatoes and manioc in with the leftover rice to have enough to eat. Looking back on my life there, I feel good. I was so innocent. If I'd lived in a big city, I'd have learned more. I didn't learn much there. My world was the mountains, streams, rice fields, banana and coconut trees. I grew up like a tomboy. I cut my hair short, went swimming and running, and climbed trees. People were always friendly to me. I helped people a lot. In school I'd give poorer kids rice and money so they could contribute to the school festival. Sometimes I'd steal rice from my grandparents so I could give it to poor kids." She laughed. "I don't think that's such a bad thing to do."

Quyen left school in the ninth grade. "I had to leave because of the paperwork for the Amerasian program. When the Homecoming Program started, one of my grandparents' friends in Saigon heard about it and let us know. People had started buying Amerasians so they could get out of Vietnam. She came to our house—all the way from Saigon to our little village! She was very rich and already had a daughter in the U.S. She told my grandparents she'd help my mother and me to get out. She and her husband would pretend to be our parents; they'd say my mother was my older sister. In Saigon, if you have money and know the system, you can get fake birth certificates. The woman said if we'd do it, she'd give my grandparents her house in Saigon. Then she started to threaten us. She said, 'you don't have any money, you won't be able to get the paperwork done. If you try to get out, you'll be thrown in jail.' So we kept quiet. Now I think I was dumb to believe her. Living in a small village, you just don't know much. If I'd known better, I'd have realized that my grandparents could have applied to come with us, but she and her husband ended up taking their place.

"When we got to the Philippines, they decided they didn't need us any longer. They started eating separately and ignoring us. I felt angry because we were helping them to come here. Finally I decided to tell the authorities the truth. The night before I did, I stayed up all night worrying. I felt very conflicted about telling them. I'd lied to the authorities in Vietnam, telling them the woman was my mother. Now I was afraid they'd keep us in the Philippines or send us back to Vietnam. When I did tell, the authorities thought I was crazy. They had me see a psychologist. He asked me a lot of questions. I told him I'd lied before when I said those other people were my parents. I showed him my father's photograph. I asked him to write a letter to find my father. Apparently he did, because a month later my father called the Philippines and they let me go to the U.S. Otherwise they'd have kept me there because they thought I had psychological problems. In the Philippines a lot of Amerasians tried to separate from the people who had bought them.

"My father and his family came to meet me and my mother at the airport. He was with his wife, my half sister, and two of his wife's children from a previous marriage. He's been married three times. My half sister is older than I am. He'd had her before going to Vietnam. I didn't know how to act; the culture in the U.S. is different from the culture in Vietnam. I saw people at the airport hugging each other, so I hugged him. I was scared and nervous. I didn't know if he was really my father. I had his picture, but I couldn't tell if it was really him. He had a hard time with me for the first few months. I didn't know how to act and I was always crying. I cried because I felt. . . . I don't know how I felt. I was just so uncomfortable. He wanted me to live with him and his wife, and for my mother to live by herself, so he could get to know me. He tried to make up to me for the past, but I didn't want it. I did live with him for a few months while my mother lived with a friend. We didn't have enough money to rent an apartment on our own. There were a lot of problems."

I asked Quyen if she could describe her present relationship with her father. "We're closer and closer every day, yet I still feel like I could live without him, but not without my mother. American parents behave differently than Vietnamese parents; there isn't as much love or sense of responsibility. He bought a car for me, but I had to pay for part of it. I understood that he was married and had a family, so I didn't say anything. I think he should have paid the whole thing. I have to pay my tuition, buy my clothes, everything. I feel he should have done more. Maybe his wife complained. In Vietnam parents do everything for their children until they finish school. He wasn't there for me when I was young. When I came here, I didn't feel like he did enough for me, but I didn't complain. I didn't want to make trouble." I asked Quyen how she feels about her father now. She said, "I love him." Then she began to cry. I asked if she feels anything toward him besides love. She continued to cry as she responded. "I wonder why this has happened to me? Why does he care for other people's children—his wife's—but not for me, his own baby? Even though I'm grown up, I feel it's his responsibility. It hurts my feelings. He says, 'you're old enough to care for yourself.' I never talk to him about how I really feel. I have friends at school. Their parents do everything for them and I think, 'why did this happen to me?' But I never tell them how I feel. Nobody knows I'm sad. Nobody knows I have a problem. At work, I tell everyone he loves me and cares for me.

"I don't see him much anymore. We're getting farther and farther apart every day; the distance is growing. He promised he'd pay my tuition and take care of me, but that wasn't true. I know he loves me, but love is not enough. He should support me. Love, you can say it, but what you do is the proof. Compared to my mother, he only gives 10 percent. But I don't want people to know about my family problems. I want them to think I'm happy." I asked Quyen if there is anyone she can talk to about how she really feels. "Sometimes I talk with my best friend. She also has trouble with her father. But I always try to look happy. People treat me well, I'm busy, so I don't think about what's happened in my family." I asked when she had first begun to feel sad. "The sadness started when I came here. Life is so hard. I have to adjust to school and the language. The sadness is about starting all over again. I keep it in my heart and don't talk about it. I want to go to school, get a good job, and be successful so my mom can stop working. She's had a hard life taking care of my family and me. I hate the war. The war caused my problems and so many problems for so many people. I pray every day, no more war."

After our interview, I told Quyen I was sorry she felt so sad and hoped she would be able to find someone with whom she could talk openly about her feelings. She responded, "it's good to talk; it's a relief." Her mother had been watching us while we talked, and I noticed that her eyes, too, were filled with tears. We said our good-byes and left. Walking back to the car, the interpreter and I were silent for a while. Then I said, "she's really a lovely girl. She has suffered so much. It's as if her life has been one betrayal after the other." The interpreter, a Vietnamese woman who has experienced a great deal of suffering in her own life, responded, "I found a real soul mate in her mother. We talked about the war and all that we had endured both there and here. She's a strong, sensitive person. I've arranged to meet with her again. I think we could become good friends."

Under a facade of cheerfulness, Quyen felt disappointed and unhappy. "Why has this happened to me?" It is a question I have heard many Amerasians ask, a protest against the circumstances that make their lives so difficult. Why had their fathers abandoned them? Why have people discriminated against them for the accident of their birth? Why were they punished for their connection to long-ago events in which they played no part? Some try to comfort themselves with the traditional Vietnamese belief in karma. They imagine they must have done something wrong in a past life and are being punished for it in the present. Once their karmic debt is paid, they believe they will be reborn into a happier life. Others, like Quyen, try to hide their sadness and anger and to convert them into more acceptable feelings, such as a concern for the needs and well-being of others. It is no accident that

Quyen decided to become a nurse. In part it is an attempt to identify with that aspect of her father she can love and respect—the pilot who rescued the wounded. It is also a way to give to others the care and compassion she so desperately wants for herself.

Quyen's sadness and anger appear to derive in part from conflicting cultural expectations for the behavior of parents toward children and children toward parents. Quyen's American father seems to expect his daughter to become increasingly independent of him—she should help pay for her car and get a job to pay for her tuition. As a Vietnamese, Quyen expects to remain dependent on him until her studies are complete. American parents, like those in other developed Western societies, seek to promote *in*dependence in their children. Giving flows one way, from parent to child, tapering off as the child reaches maturity, and with no expectation that the gift will be repaid. Vietnamese parents, on the other hand, promote *inter*dependence.[1] Parents care for children until they are on their own, then expect reciprocal caretaking when they, the parents, are old.

In addition, however, Quyen's wish to be more dependent on her father stems from an understandable belief that her early dependency needs—for a father's love and support—were not met. At some level she seems to expect repayment for the many years during which she and her mother suffered so much because her father abandoned them.

The complex feelings and expectations—both individually and culturally based—that underlie the relationships between Amerasians and their fathers may help explain why their reunions are so often unsuccessful. The emotional debt accumulated after many years of deprivation and neglect is simply too large to be completely repaid. While they are genetically related, Amerasians and their fathers are people from vastly different worlds. It is unlikely that they will ever fully understand one another.

1. Jerome Kagan, *The Nature of the Child* (New York: Basic Books, 1984).

Conclusion

WHEN I ASKED AMERASIANS STILL IN VIETNAM WHAT THEY
wanted me to convey to the American people, they responded with
passion and near despair.

"Tell them we want to get out of Vietnam as soon as possible,
before it's too late. It's our only chance to be educated and useful and
to have a better life."

"Is there any way you can help us? Can you raise a voice for the
Amerasians of Vietnam? We are fatherless. If we said something wrong
in the ODP interview it's because we are confused about our past lives.
Please ask the Americans to be generous and accept us. We are victims
of the war. We've lost many things. We have no father, no mother,
and no relatives. How can they turn us away?"

"I am a Vietnamese Amerasian. Other Amerasians are allowed to go
to the U.S.; why not me? I should have that right, too. If they'll let me
go, I'll work hard to make a future for my children and earn money to
send back to my foster mother. She is very poor. If I stay here, I'll be
too poor to help her. In Vietnam I've suffered a lot for being Amerasian. I just want to get out. Americans need to understand that Vietnamese despise Amerasians. Most of us have never experienced love

and affection. Our society rejects us. As a result, many of us are angry. We get upset at what has happened to us and sometimes we misbehave. People should try to understand our situation and not blame us for being human."

"Please ask the U.S. government to change its mind about us and let us go to our fatherland. We've suffered so much over the last twenty years. I know I'm the child of an American. Every time I see an American, I wonder if he's my father. Please raise a voice for us."

"All Amerasians want to resettle in the United States. From the day we were born, the constant discrimination in Vietnam has made our lives awful. When we go for ODP interviews they keep asking for information about our fathers and for documentation. But after Liberation Day everyone burned their papers! They were terrified about what would happen if the government knew they'd been with the Americans. Now the ODP asks us all these questions. If we get mixed up, they deny our application. I have nothing at all back in my village. My mother's house has collapsed, and my relatives there are very old and can't support us. If we're turned out of here, we'll have nowhere to go, no place to live. We'll be street people. We've suffered all our lives, and we just want to get out of here."

What I have tried to convey in these pages is a picture of what it was and is like to be a Vietnamese Amerasian. In doing so, I hope to reawaken the compassion of people in the United States for these, their children, abandoned long ago in Vietnam. I also hope to interest people in other parts of the world in these survivors of poverty, racism, and neglect, and to illustrate through their lives the importance of protecting children who are victims of war, political conflict, and discrimination. The Amerasians who made it out of Vietnam and now live in the land of their fathers are generally doing well. They are not rich or famous, but they are survivors who have learned to cope with adversity and make the most of what is available to them. The Amerasians who remain in Vietnam are frightened and bitter that the door to a better life in the United States is about to close for good. Abandoned once before by their fathers and the American government, they fear that they are about to be abandoned again.

To be a Vietnamese Amerasian in postwar Vietnam was to be a child growing up in the hands of your father's enemies. The hatred that the enemy had felt, and continued to feel, for your father and his country was directed against you, even though you were innocent of any wrongdoing. You were treated with scorn and derision by many of those around you who hated you for the way you looked and for what you, in their minds, represented. You were denied the love and support of a father who left you behind often before he even knew you. Sometimes you were also denied a mother's love, and were passed around from person to person, and place to place, until you found a home with strangers. You were denied the opportunity to continue your schooling and to exercise your talents and abilities to their full extent. You became an outcast in a land that was not really your home, but was the only home you knew. Yet, despite it all, you survived. If you were fortunate, you found people to love you and teach you how to love yourself. You went to school for as long as your family's poverty, the taunting of your classmates, or the policies of the Vietnamese government would let you. You searched for work, often doing the jobs no one else wanted to do, or traveled far from home to places where work was available. You fell in love and began to raise a family, often having children who, like you, looked more like the people in a distant land than the people among whom you lived.

Are there universal lessons we can learn from the Vietnamese Amerasian experience? I believe there are.

1. Fathers should bear the responsibility for their children. If the fathers are soldiers, the nation they represent must reinforce that responsibility and accept the children, from the beginning of their lives,

as its own. The behavior of many American soldiers and the U.S. government toward their children in Vietnam was often irresponsible and condemned those children to lives of poverty, prejudice, and discrimination. The decision to bring the Amerasians home, in their teens, twenties, and thirties, was the right thing to do, but it came too late in their lives to offer them a full and unlimited potential for development. The Amerasians, and their mothers, should have been accepted as the responsibility of the United States from the beginning, and all who wanted to come to the United States during and after the war should have been allowed to do so.

2. The long-term, continuous presence and love of a mother, or her surrogate, in the early years of a child's life is critical to the child's development of a capacity to love him- or herself and others. As illustrated in the lives of many Amerasians, a mother's love also appears to offer some protection against adversity. Amerasians who did not enjoy their mother's love and continuous presence during their early years were able to cope and adapt to life in Vietnam and the United States, but often they seemed to me to be unhappy human beings who did not feel good about themselves. Governments should recognize the central importance of a loving, continuous relationship with a mother or mother-surrogate and reinforce that relationship legally and economically. The U.S. government's abandonment of Amerasians and their mothers in postwar Vietnam sentenced them to lives of poverty and prejudice, allowing a situation to develop in which some mothers felt they had no choice but to abandon their children. The decision to impose the postwar trade embargo further exacerbated this situation, crippling Vietnam economically and creating renewed hatred of the United States. This resulted in a further decline in the living conditions of America's children, its former South Vietnamese allies, and their children, continuing and increasing the Vietnamese government's mistreatment of people the U.S. government should have been trying to protect.

3. Human beings have a remarkable capacity to cope with adversity.

Despite the many obstacles confronting them, Amerasians survived and struggled to build better lives for themselves. This adaptability, however, should not become an excuse for individuals and governments to practice neglect, assuming that human injustices will somehow correct themselves.

Having abandoned the Amerasians as children, would it have been better to leave them as young adults in Vietnam, where they at least understood and shared in the culture and had some social support? In the eight years I have been working with Amerasians I have met very few who, for more than a fleeting moment of despair, seriously wanted to leave the United States and return to Vietnam. As little as many of them have in the United States, they have far more than they ever had or could hope to have in Vietnam. At a minimum they have adequate shelter, food, and clothing, and can send their children to school to get the education most of them were denied.

Now that the harm has been done, and Amerasians' potential for growth and development has been severely limited by time and neglect, most are undoubtedly better off in the United States than in Vietnam. Once they are here, however, it is important that we not forget them again. Along with other immigrants and refugees from non-English-speaking backgrounds, the most important thing we can provide Amerasians in the United States is the opportunity to learn English well. Although some attempts are made to teach them English, both at the Philippine Refugee Processing Center and at cluster sites in the United States, few receive adequate language training. Given their limited educational backgrounds in Vietnam, Amerasians require intensive, full-time, and often long-term English language courses. Unfortunately, government policies limiting the length of time they can receive welfare benefits after arrival mean that most must go to work before their English language skills are adequate to get more than menial jobs. Enabling Amerasians to study English full time for at least the first year after arrival would enlarge the vocational opportunities available to them, decrease long-term welfare dependence, and reduce their isolation from mainstream America.

And what about the Amerasians still in Vietnam? During my last trip to the Transit Center in 1997 I met many young Vietnamese claiming to be Amerasians who, in my opinion, truly were children of Americans. All wanted desperately to come to the United States. In recent years, however, it has become increasingly difficult for Amerasian applicants and their families to gain acceptance into the Resettlement Program. The reasons for this apparent shift in U.S. government policy toward them are not entirely clear. My knowledge of the variables involved in the Amerasian selection process is largely second or third hand and anecdotal. While I do have U.S. State Department documents describing how the interview and selection process is supposed to work, these were produced early in the Resettlement Program's history and may not reflect more recent U.S. government policy. Transit Center officials with whom I spoke seemed to place the blame for declining acceptance rates on U.S. interviewers' wariness at being defrauded by "fake" Amerasians and their families. They believed that the interviewers had become overly suspicious and exclusive, rejecting people who really were Amerasians for the slightest inconsistency or discrepancy in their or their family's story. The Amerasians themselves tended to single out specific interviewers as being especially tough and unforgiving. For example, there was one man they referred to as "Mr. Ten Percent" because he reportedly approved only 10 percent of applications. My impression is that the change in acceptance rates was the consequence of several factors: U.S. government concern about immigration fraud; decreasing political support for the Amerasian Resettlement Program; a general lack of interest among the American public toward immigrants and refugees ("compassion fatigue"); and perhaps, the cynical views of certain interviewers toward anyone claiming to be Amerasian.

How might this difficult situation be remedied? Having worked with thousands of Amerasians over the past eight years, Transit Center staff, and especially Mr. Thien and Mrs. Lien Tam, could be of enormous assistance in helping U.S. officials separate "true" from "fake" Amerasians and their families. Working collaboratively with them, the U.S. government might carefully and speedily review the cases of all persons claiming to be Amerasian and their relatives who wish to enter the United States. In my opinion, it would be far better to err on the side of letting in a few more "fake" Amerasians and family members than to exclude any of those who really are America's children and wish to come home at last.

Glossary

Amerasian Transit Center: The Amerasian Transit Center, located in Ho Chi Minh City, Vietnam, was built with American funds and opened in 1990. It provided accommodation for Amerasians and their families awaiting U.S. immigration interviews, physical exams, and inclusion on flight manifests for transportation to Manila and the Philippine Refugee Processing Center.

Cyclo: Often referred to as a "pedicab," a cyclo is a bicycle modified by having a passenger seat attached in front in place of the front wheel and supported on either side by bicycle tires. These human-powered taxis continue to function as a primary form of transportation for people and goods in large cities such as Ho Chi Minh City and Hanoi.

Dust of life (*bui doi*): This expression refers to the poorest of the poor, not specifically to Amerasians.

Manioc: a tuberous, starchy plant, similar to tapioca, which is sometimes eaten as a snack and may also be consumed as a primary food if rice is not available.

Montagnards: Hill tribes of various ethnic groups who occupy mountainous regions along Vietnam's borders with Cambodia, China, and Laos. Some of these tribes fought along with the United States and its allies during the Vietnam War.

My-lai: literally "American half-breed," a term used to refer to Vietnamese Amerasians.

New Economic Zones (NEZ): Previously unsettled or sparsely settled regions in Vietnam to which former South Vietnamese military and officials, their families, Amerasians, and others were sent as settlers to expand Vietnam's cultivatable land and reduce urban crowding.

Orderly Departure Program (ODP): The Orderly Departure Program was established by the United States government in 1979 to deal with the flood of people leaving Vietnam as boat people. It offered Vietnamese the opportunity to emigrate to the United States safely and legally. Beginning in 1982, Amerasians were also permitted to emigrate under the ODP. With passage of the Amerasian Homecoming Act in 1987, Amerasians continued to be processed under the Orderly Departure Program as one of three subprograms. The other two subprograms were for former political prisoners and for persons with close family ties in the United States.

Philippine Refugee Processing Center (PRPC): Located north of Manila on the Bataan peninsula, the PRPC is a large refugee camp through which many thousands of Southeast Asians, including Vietnamese Amerasians, passed on their way to the United States and other countries. Vietnamese Amerasians generally stayed at the PRPC for six months, studying English and learning about American culture and work habits.

PX: "Post exchange," the military equivalent of a combined super-market and department store in the United States, where military personnel and their dependents can buy goods at much reduced prices.

Saigon/Ho Chi Minh City: Saigon was the former name for Ho Chi Minh City prior to its fall to the Communists. Many people in Vietnam continue to use the two names interchangeably, although Ho Chi Minh City is the formal name used in government communications and documents.

Viet Cong: Literally, "Vietnamese Communists," the term used by Americans and their allies to refer to Communist guerrilla forces operating in South Vietnam and to persons in the South who adhered to the Communist cause. The Communists referred to themselves as the National Liberation Front.

Bibliography

Those who wish to read more about Vietnamese Amerasians, about traditional Vietnamese life and culture, or about the experiences of other child victims of war are referred to the following publications.

Apfel, Roberta J., and Bennett Simon, eds. *Minefields in Their Hearts: The Mental Health of Children in War and Communal Violence.* New Haven: Yale University Press, 1996.

Bass, Thomas A. *Vietnamerica: The War Comes Home.* New York: Soho Press, 1996.

Bemak, Fred, and Rita Chi-Ying C. Chung. "Vietnamese Amerasians: Psychosocial Adjustment and Psychotherapy." *Journal of Multicultural Counseling and Development* 25 (1997): 79–88.

Federal Research Division of the Library of Congress. *Vietnam: A Country Study.* Washington, D.C.: U.S. Government Printing Office, 1989.

Felsman, J. Kirk, et al. "Estimates of Psychological Distress among Vietnamese Refugees: Adolescents, Unaccompanied Minors, and Young Adults." *Social Science and Medicine* 31 (1985): 1251–56.

————. *Vietnamese Amerasians: Practical Implications of Current Research*. Washington, D.C.: Office of Refugee Resettlement, Department of Health and Human Services, 1989.

Graham, Philip. "Prevention." In *Child and Adolescent Psychiatry: Modern Approaches*. Ed. Michael Rutter et al. 3rd ed. (pp. 815–16). London: Blackwell, 1994.

Hickey, Gerald Cannon. *Village in Vietnam*. New Haven: Yale University Press, 1964.

Houtart, Francois, and Genevieve Lemercinier. *Hai Van: Life in a Vietnamese Commune*. London: Zed Books, 1984.

Jamieson, Neil L. *Understanding Vietnam*. Berkeley: University of California Press, 1993.

Leong, Frederick T. L., and Mark C. Johnson. *Vietnamese Amerasian Mothers: Psychological Distress and High-Risk Factors*. Washington, D.C.: Office of Refugee Resettlement, Department of Health and Human Services, 1992.

McKelvey, Robert S., Alice R. Mao, and John A. Webb. "A Risk Profile Predicting Psychological Distress in Vietnamese Amerasian Youth." *Journal of the American Academy of Child and Adolescent Psychiatry* 31 (1992): 911–15.

————. "Premigratory Expectations and Mental Health Symptoms in a Group of Vietnamese Amerasian Youth." *Journal of the American Academy of Child and Adolescent Psychiatry* 32 (1993): 414–18.

McKelvey, Robert S., and John A. Webb. "Long-Term Effects of Maternal Loss on Vietnamese Amerasians." *Journal of the American Academy of Child and Adolescent Psychiatry* 32 (1993): 1013–18.

――――. "Unaccompanied Status as a Risk Factor in Vietnamese Amerasians." *Social Science and Medicine* 41 (1995): 261–66.

――――. "Premigratory Expectations and Postmigratory Mental Health." *Journal of the American Academy of Child and Adolescent Psychiatry* 35 (1996): 240–45.

――――. "A Comparative Study of Amerasians, Their Siblings, and Unrelated Like-Aged Vietnamese." *American Journal of Psychiatry* 153 (1996): 561–63.

McKelvey, Robert S., John A. Webb, and Alice R. Mao. "Premigratory Risk Factors in Vietnamese Amerasians." *American Journal of Psychiatry* 150 (1993): 470–73.

Nwadiora, Emeka, and Harriette McAdoo. "Acculturative Stress among Amerasian Refugees: Gender and Racial Differences." *Adolescence* 31 (1996): 477–87.

Pran, Dith. *Children of Cambodia's Killing Fields: Memoirs of Survivors.* New Haven: Yale University Press, 1997.

United States Catholic Conference. *In Our Fathers' Land: Vietnamese Amerasians in the United States.* Washington, D.C.: United States Catholic Conference, 1985.

United States General Accounting Office. *Vietnamese Amerasian Resettlement: Education, Employment, and Family Outcomes in the United*

States. Washington, D.C.: United States General Accounting Office, 1994.

Valverde, Kieu-Linh Caroline. "From Dust to Gold: The Vietnamese Amerasian Experience." In *Racially Mixed People in America.* Ed. Maria P. P. Root (pp. 144–61). Newbury Park, Calif.: Sage Publications, 1992.

Index

ROBERT S. MCKELVEY, M.D., is Professor and Director of the Division of Child and Adolescent Psychiatry at the Oregon Health Sciences University in Portland, Oregon. From 1995 to 1998 he was Foundation Professor of Child Psychiatry at the University of Western Australia in Perth. *(Photograph by David Sharbanee. The author at the War Memorial in King's Park, Perth, Western Australia.)*